WHAT THEY
THE AL

CW01433705

Over the last three decades, Dean Fraser has become one of the world's leading advocates of dowsing as a means of connecting to our own intuition and is also a passionate teacher of meditation and holistic lifestyles – PSYCHIC NEWS

The author's quest for metaphysical growth has seen him travel across two continents in search of truth, network with fellow seekers of enlightenment and visit sacred sites to attune with their energies – BODYMINDSOUL.COM

Dean was very interactive with the audience afterwards and from that, he has offered to come back to do a session on how to meditate. A direct request from the audience – EVENT HOST

Dean sees his mission in life to spread some much-needed laughter and love in this world - INDIE SHAMAN MAGAZINE

Published Worldwide in 2025

This first edition published 2025

ISBN 9798343841978

NOBODY ASKED ME IF I WANTED TO BE PSYCHIC!

The life of a spiritual healer and
paranormal investigator

Dean Fraser

CONTENTS

Dedicated to Yew Tree pioneer and visionary
Alan Meredith

PROLOGUE

Aged two we went to visit my grandparents. Nana had a migraine headache. She sat there in her chair looking unhappy and asking us all to please be quiet. I looked at her and reaching-up spontaneously placed my hands on her forehead. She winced but humoured me to see what would happen next. Ten minutes later to her amazement she declared her headache gone!

Over the next few years I would become in demand around the family if anyone had a headache or any other kind of pain. Laying on of my hands seemed to work for whoever I was helping, at least to some extent.

I honestly thought everyone did this. When I came of school age to discover this being far from the case I was shocked. I also soon learned to keep quiet about hands-on healing or else face accusations of witchcraft from my classmates.

GROWING UP AND GROWING IN A HAUNTED HOUSE

I never dreamt of being a paranormal investigator or psychic healer. When I was little and well-meaning

7

adults would ask me what I wanted to be when I grew up I would reply that I was going to be an actor. I read about it for many hours every week. When reaching my teens it became too obvious I was something of a natural writer and performer. My dream of acting for a living got replaced with a love of writing and public speaking instead. These days I write for around thirty magazines each year and devote many days to sharing my story with others at live events.

With inevitability investigating hauntings and offering psychic healing also became my reality. After all this has been practically a part of who I am since was a toddler. This book is your personal invite to enter alongside me into my world, where the weird and downright bizarre is commonplace. You may find that you never view your own safe world in quite the same way again!

You will have more than likely enjoyed those television series or vlogs following paranormal investigators on cases. There is a wealth of hi-tech kit available out there to help in ghost detection and psychic communication. Some of these high-profile teams or individuals utilize all of them and then yet others eschew these electronic aids altogether to rely more on their intuition or psychic ability.

Similarly, we have all seen footage of those exorcising people of elemental energy or cleansing a property of its unwanted resident entity. Again, here we see bibles and/or crosses, incantations chanted in Latin, sage smudging or any one of the myriads of other tools and methods used to achieve the desired objective.

As this is a question which comes up countless times to elicit my consistently response; allow me to share with you right now the inner secrets to my own personal ghost hunting kit. My kit is to all intents and purposes me!

I frequently use 'trigger objects' to help connect to spirit entities. Trigger objects include personal items relating to an individual and over the years even donning a gas mask to align myself with any spirits who lived when these were in common use, during the wars of the last century. Then there are those occasions I have totally immersed myself in a bygone era in my quest to uncover more…but those are stories for another book. This time we look at cases taken directly from my several decades of activity.

Often helping with insight into a distant healing or locating a particularly pernicious entity wishing to elude me I consult with my dowsing pendulum for a little metaphysical feedback. I came into dowsing from an active interest in tarot cards and astrology. I wanted a quicker method for gaining insights into the unknown and more immediate answers to my many questions. Pendulum dowsing proved to be the perfect solution.

The rest though is down to all my decades of experience and a finely honed intuitive sense of dealing with the situation using the most effective method I sense will work. I use no other kit and actually never have done.

I require a good working knowledge of history for my investigations to be effective and to this end I have read many history textbooks over the years.

To protect their identity, the real names of those I helped have been changed. The same with locations, unless they are central to the story, street and building names have also been altered to protect the privacy of those now living or working there.

What I have done for anyone curious enough is to leave a few cryptic breadcrumbs for you to follow regarding my haunted locations. But do be careful if you care and dare to follow in my footsteps, you should know that I use extremely strong psychic self-protection built upon over several decades. You have been duly warned…

This book contains true stories as transcribed from my personal paranormal diaries. I also share some cases of me offering distant healing, sometimes from thousands of miles away and releasing people from potentially life-threatening emotional blockages.

Here we have dark tales of demonic entities taken on in world famous Megalithic monuments, through to cases of ghosts found lurking in apparently perfectly ordinary homes, sat there on equally ordinary suburban streets.

I lived in the paranormal portal that is Chretien Road from being four to nine years old. That the experiences still remains so fresh in my memory all these years later is indicative of just exactly how weird and of-the-scale haunted that place was!

Originally I intended to co-author this book with my mother, after all she also lived through many of these events and quite a few I didn't witness. She was able to make light of some of this weirdness to me as a child to protect me a little from getting too freaked-out and still be able to sleep. She also personally knew as friends our paranormally savvy eccentric neighbours Olive and Joe. The couple who were to end up central to so many of these stories of our time in Chretien Road, which will be related exactly as they occurred in the following pages.

Fate took a hand in things and in the end I wouldn't be able to co-author this with my mother, she unfortunately passed away a little over five years ago after an illness. Although it has taken me a few years to find enough spare time to write this book, as a lifelong psychic, I know for sure that my mother still acts out her role as consultant as I finally pen this book, overseeing me and ensuring that I get all my facts right!

Many other arcane experiences happened and continue to happen in my life, but my early childhood certainly set the scene for all that was to follow, so I invite you come with me and visit the past as we together explore Chretien Road...but first a word about Spiritual Healing.

HEALING FOR OTHERS

The ethics of healing are rarely straightforward. I will never embark upon a healing treatment for anyone who has not directly asked me to help them. Ever!

This has proved a personal challenge on so many levels throughout my life when faced with the stark reality of those I deeply care about and love going through some life-changing or indeed life-ending challenge. Yet I know I have absolutely no right to intervene unless asked.

It is unconditionally their right to pass through these challenges; however they ultimately play-out.

CRYSTALS FOUND ME

I got my first introduction to the power of crystals in the early 1990's. Until then I confess, although already an avid student of metaphysics, crystals were not really something I had given too much thought to.

The first mystical book I read was Linda Goodman's Star Signs, in this book she did recommend specific crystals to align with our Zodiac Sign. Yet at that point I never felt inclined to explore for myself why that might be. A paradigm shift awaited me...

My introduction to crystals effectively came as a result of my dowsing. I read books. And I really do mean a lot of books! I still read, but nothing like at the level of intensity I did back then. I absorbed all of this new-to-me knowledge like the proverbial sponge.

By and by I commenced reading the extensive series of books written about and based around the readings of somnambulist mystic Edgar Cayce. Working my way through these writings I found myself intrigued by his frequent mentions of the power of gems and crystals. Particularly fascinating to me were crystals and their connection with the lost lands of Atlantis and Lemuria.

My interest suitably piqued, my next project became to learn more of these crystals and what bringing them into my own life might do for me. In those days before the internet, finding metaphysical suppliers meant buying the kinds of magazines they might be found to advertise in. Such a magazine showed there to be a crystal shop located around an hour's drive from me. Off I went to see what I would see.

I recognised some of the crystals from all the books I had been reading. I bought an amethyst cluster, a rose quartz tumblestone and a quartz point. Little did I know what awaited me!

This visit to that little crystal shop acted as the catalyst for all that was to follow. A years or so later I started a wholesale business, namely The Strawberry Crystal, designing my range of Crystal Healing and Pendulum Dowsing Kits, supplying retailers across two continents.

A few years later, as my reputation spread, I got invited to give talks at spiritual centres on the healing power of crystals. I found myself enjoying sharing my enthusiasm for crystals with an interested audience more personally rewarding than running a business, eventually I made what turned out to the easy choice, to close my business and focus all my energy on delivering talks as my future career.

LUCID DREAMING AND A QUARRY

In the late 1990's I started to experience strong lucid dreams.

In these particular lucid dreams I continually saw a quarry. Specifically I saw myself in this quarry looking for a stone. The stone in question was a small piece of pure copper ore. The quarry, according to my lucid dream was once a centre of bronze-age activity but had fallen from mass collective memory to become forgotten.

I could no longer ignore this urging from my Higher Self and I decided to dowse. I dowsed over maps, until I found the place, which turned out to be situated in Staffordshire, England. I travelled there the next day. Walking with my eyes closed I dropped to the ground, feeling with my hands I found this piece of copper ore. This is actually my most powerful healing stone and travels with me everywhere I go in my pocket – over the decades this little stone has visited countless countries across two continents.

A case of never judging by appearance, my copper ore is not particularly aesthetically pleasing, being composed of copper though it is of the goddess and additionally as I know it was a personal gift to me from Mother Earth (Gaia), doubly so. My most prized crystal!

A PERSONAL INVITE

I never run from unexplained creepy banging noises or weird shadow figures. I will generally sprint headlong towards them! And now come take my hand and walk (or perhaps more accurately run!) alongside me into my paranormal world...

DARK FORCES ATTACK THE TODDLER

We were going out for a picnic when suddenly the demon swooped down to devour me...

****

I admit I could be called a strange three-year-old and in many ways mature beyond my years, people told me they felt I looked into their soul when I stared at them. I am not sure I really did, but for sure I could feel if they were unwell. The incident I relate here is one of many childhood encounters with unexplainable phenomena.

We were going out for the day to enjoy a picnic, adult preparation being well underway, given my three-year-old impatience to set-off, my parents suggested why don't I go and wait in the car then they would be out to join me in a moment. The car in question sat out on our driveway, and so it was I climbed up onto the back seat to wait for hopefully not too long.

Looking around, as I knelt up on the seat, I suddenly found myself transfixed by a massive taloned flying creature swooping down out of nowhere! The creature headed straight for the back window of the car I was sat in...

Sheer panic overtook me as I grabbed for the door-handle, which thankfully my small fingers quickly found, as I leapt out of the car to sprint straight back into the house in sheer terror. I am not sure quite what my parents made of all this; anyway at some point I must have calmed down enough for us to be able to resume our day out. After then I kept one eye on the back-window for quite a while whenever I travelled in the car;

and as a child never volunteered to wait anywhere in any car on my own again!

From the momentary glimpse, if you asked me to now describe this creature which is indelibly imprinted upon my subconscious, I would say it was larger than any bird native to the UK, with brown feathers, long talons, red eyes and possessed of an enormous wingspan. And definite intelligence, it looked me straight in the eyes as it swooped down towards me.

I do have the impression looking back that its intention had been to scare me (mission certainly accomplished!). I guess should it have wished me any true harm I would not have been able to defend myself against it in any practical way.

I felt for many years after that this creature was most likely to have been demonic in nature. Yet meditating upon the encounter more recently brings me instead to the conclusion it was considerably more likely to have been some kind of flying elemental. As I mentioned, had it been demonic in nature it certainly would not have left me alone when I fled. And I never encountered it again. Which, similarly, if the creature had been more demonic it would hardly have simply given up the hunt. With my now considerable experience with elemental and faery beings I am inclined to believe this is what I witnessed that day.

From an early age I could sense if people were unwell, to offer hands-on healing for my family without inhibition. I genuinely thought everyone did this and found myself quite shocked as I grew a little older to discover this was far from the case.

All in all, I suppose I was the classic naturally psychic small child. This was to prove both a blessing and a something of a personal challenge once I found myself living in Chretien Road...

UNSEEN HANDS PUSH RUSSELL OFF HIS BIKE

We all enjoyed playing out on our bikes, the quiet cul-de-sac affording us the run of the road in addition to the pavement. Russell was a couple of years older than me and could ride like the wind or at least it seemed that way to my then six-year-old self. Unfortunately this being Chretien Road situations had a way of changing in a second. Russell would visit hospital before the day was through...

****

If you have been reading this book in order you will have already seen a reference to my time spent living in the infamous Chretien Road in my Foreword.

Allow me to share with you the tale of Russell; and in next chapter The Stinking Demon, yet another weirdly true story illustrating exactly what kind of a paranormal portal we all lived in back in those days.

This crisp winter's day was certainly cold, yet dry, and as usual all of us children had taken the opportunity to play out on our bikes. At first there were only three of us, but as other children heard our noisy enjoyment, out they came to join in and naturally I suppose at some point we all attempted to see how fast we might cover the entire length of our cul-de-sac.

Chretien Road was a cul-de-sac and remained nicely free of passing cars, if any neighbour needed to exit or enter their driveway we all dutifully moved over to the side of the road and thereafter resumed with our bike racing adventures.

Up and down we rode our bikes day in and day out. And it was safe. Or so we thought…

Russell joined in after we had already been playing for an hour or so. I liked him a lot. Although bigger than me, he remained consistently kind and patient with us smaller children. In fact, of our entire bicycle posse he was probably the nicest, always inclusive in his play and encouraging to those not as able as himself.

I followed just behind Russell as we furiously peddled past my own home and down towards his own at the head of the cul-de-sac. When suddenly with no warning both rider and bike fell violently to the left, making hard unforgiving contact with the road!

I was positioned directly behind Russell when this all happened. He hadn't turned or lost his balance, simply tipped over to the left in all but a moment.

Russell, in shock I suppose, didn't cry out or shout…the steady stream of blood running down his face from the gash in his forehead did understandably prompt some of the other smaller children to cry though. Running as fast as I was able, I banged hard upon the front door of his parent's house and off Russell went to hospital for stitches.

Russell talked to us all later that same day and described feeling like he was pushed hard off his bike by unseen hands. His family thought he must have wobbled when turning, he was adamant his handlebars were straight when he came off and being right there within a metre of him when it happened I confirmed he had indeed ridden in a straight line. Suddenly, and for no apparent reason, Russell fell violently to the left, ending up in a crumpled mess of bike and rider in the middle of the road.

Russell happily made a full physical recovery, however understandably never did show any further enthusiasm for bike riding in Chretien Road.

THE STINKING DEMON

Was there a demonic presence lurking in Chretien Road taking pleasure in attacking the innocent or unwary?

****

Looking back with the benefit of my considerable adult experience, absolutely there was at least one demon and more than likely several of them causing their mayhem completely independently of one another!

I now call forward someone who lived there at that time. One credible eyewitness right there on the spot and who experienced the manifestation of a demon inside a house there in Chretien Road. Me!

It was the disgusting smell we noticed firstly. Likened to the sulphur of matches mixed with the overpowering animal odour of skunk. We had a cat called Fluffy and she would suddenly turn uncharacteristically aggressive for no apparent reason, hissing and spitting in anger at some area of the room and then with her bravery levels reached, off she would sprint upstairs to hide. And we eventually started to make the inevitable connection between this vile odour and our family cat having her episodes.

Neighbours also reported strange smells, even to the point of one family calling in a pest control company thinking they might have a dead rodent nest hidden somewhere in their house. Of course, nothing was found.

In our home this phenomenon continued for several weeks and if that wasn't enough, suddenly things got far less easy to ignore. We were to be horrified when there commenced a significant step-up in activity...

I wasn't the only person to see this demonic creature. All of our independently written and yet matching descriptions across the neighbourhood corroborated we were collectively witnessing the same entity. And for some reason it now decided to manifest, to physically make itself known to us!

About the size of a small monkey, it was shiny black rather like the carapace of a beetle and the impression is it would be hard to the touch (not that any of us actually gave that one a go!). It crouched low to the ground, again a little like a monkey and had long arms ending in clawed hands. Ears perched on top of its head, small piercing eyes which seemed to glow red and sharp pointed teeth. The overall impression was of something utterly malevolent and evil.

Out of the corner of the eye we would glimpse it skulking along the edge of a room, accompanied by the vile aroma and for sure it was thoroughly unpleasant in every conceivable way. A few times it manifested in full view, more often than not though it would sneak around just on the edge of witness's vision, them catching only a glance in passing.

Clearly at seven years old I wasn't about to take on this entity, even if I then had the slightest idea how to. When you read later chapter My Friend Tony, more will be explained about Olive and Joe, our paranormally savvy neighbours, as they are central to that story. They also experienced this creature manifest in their own home. As it suddenly disappeared overnight (never to be seen or heard of again) I guess Joe or one of his colleagues in his psychic research group must have intervened and dealt with it.

MY FRIEND TONY

At seven years old I had finally reached year three of school. And this is when I met Tony. There he stood in the cloakroom as I hung up my coat, not quite sure what the day would bring, and he smiled at me reassuringly. He helped considerably in making me feel more secure starting that new school year and I knew there I had found a new friend...I wanted to invite him back to my house to play...yet when I talked to other children about Tony none of them knew him or even seemed to be able to see him...

****

We lived in the City of Manchester in the North of England. In common with most urban areas, the zones and suburbs were identified more in terms of villages coming together to make up the whole of the city, our village was Northenden.

We lived there before the anti-social issues that would later plague areas such as this in the next decade, and all things considered I enjoyed my life there. Close enough to Manchester City Centre, yet largely self-contained, also with a great park close by and a wonderful little library, looking back I can see exactly why my parents had chosen to live there.

Fortunately, back then the local infant school, although in a largely built-up urban area, did probably have more in common with the atmosphere of a village school rather than your typically rough and tough city school. Housed in a fine Victorian building, complete with an expansive playing field and indoor sport/assembly hall.

We lived on the edge of Northenden in Chretien Road, a quiet little cul-de-sac. The houses in this road have an interestingly compelling story to tell all of their own (which I intend to write more about in a possible future book The Ghosts Of Chretien Road) for now though I will add that one house here would become particularly relevant to this story.

Getting ready for my first day of year three, to become a participator once more in the English education system, I felt that same mixture of excitement and trepidation most of us have to go through when a new school year starts. That sense of entering into the unknown.

Setting off for school, my mother walked me the less than ten minutes to the gate and after a kiss goodbye I was on my own. We weren't allowed to cycle to school, I virtually lived on my bike so for sure would have done if permitted, school rules firmly prohibited it. Some first-timers were also being left to their fate on the same day, many with reluctant tears, old–hands such as me knew roughly what to expect.

The school bell consisted of the designated playground duty teacher of the day literally physically ringing a large handbell. At seven I couldn't really understand how quaint this was, looking back from the benefit of adult eyes, what a wonderful throw-back to a bygone era.

At 9am the bell duly rang and all of us were shepherded into the mail sports and assembly hall. For the benefit of the year ones, the head-teacher told us a little of the rules of the school and what might happen if we transgressed.

All in all though this first assembly of the school year seemed to pass on by fairly painlessly and in due course, in regimented single file, we followed our year three teacher into a different annex of the building than we had ever previously been allowed into. We had all progressed into the more grown-up area of school reserved exclusively for year's three through to six!

She showed us the classroom, next usefully where the toilets were, finally telling us to go and hang up our coats in the cloakroom, located just to the left along the corridor.

There was the usual impatient rush of children all wanting to get there first, to be quickly back to class and choose where to sit for the duration of that year in school. Next to friends or perhaps even more crucially near the radiators! As this was an old Victorian building with big high ceilings it wasn't always exactly scorching hot throughout the chillier months or more accurately absolutely freezing cold describes the average winter classroom temperature. In the 1970's there was never a question of a school closing just because we all needed to keep our coats on in class for many days throughout winter, we were simply expected to get on with it.

My experienced in matters of school etiquette seven year old self found all that dashing about and tripping over one another in their haste not really my scene. As I knew my best-friend Susan would save me a good seat next to her, I could afford to be altogether more leisurely and dignified in my approach.

I waited patiently until most the rabble had departed the cramped space of the cloakroom and entered to hang my coat on the peg I knew would be waiting there with my name written upon it. And then I encountered Tony for the first time. Stood to the rear of the cloakroom, he looked me in the eyes and smiled. He had one of those rare types of smiles which make you automatically smile back. He seemed pleased to see me smiling in return. I needed to get to my class, I said I would see him later and off I went to see exactly where Susan and I had found ourselves sitting in the end (thankfully near a radiator!).

When the morning break arrived I encountered Tony for the second time, as we all passed the cloakroom on our way to the exit door he seemed to be waiting in the corridor for me to come out of class. Out in the full light of day I was able to see him altogether better; again, we smiled at one another, as I took in the appearance of my new friend.

Although at that point I was taller than the average boy of my age (I would grow up to be 1.86 metres or six-foot one inches tall), Tony was actually bigger than me. I estimated he might already be eight or nine years old, definitely kudos to have an older friend in school. He had light brown collar length hair, obviously he wore the same kind of school uniform as all of the other boys, but he also had a distinctive mid-blue coat. It was almost knee length and looked more like a smock. No hood, pockets on either side of the coat and mittens hung from a piece of cord threaded up through the sleeves and presumably across the back. I had certainly never seen a coat quite like it. Tony was extremely pale and didn't look too healthy at all.

Walking along the short length of corridor to the welcoming freedom of the playground we talked or at least it felt like we communicated, although in hindsight

I am not entirely sure we spoke any physical words out loud.

I didn't give much thought to the matter at that age, simply accepted Tony as my friend and we talked to one another in a slightly different way than Susan and I did. He told me he felt a bit lonely and was pleased I talked with him as most often children ignored him. In return I said if he wanted, he could make friends with Susan as well and we could hang-out together at break-times. As I passed through the door out into the school yard Tony didn't follow me, in fact I had no idea where he had gone, he just wasn't there. Thinking nothing more of it, off I went on my way.

Over the next few weeks I would see Tony a few times a week, he would just sort of appear and we would have a chat, then he would go. Talking to Susan and some other friends revealed they didn't know who I was referring to when I mentioned Tony, and more tellingly they never saw us together. The exact nature of Tony was a bit of a mystery to me, when I mentioned him, I am sure some of my friends and family felt I invented an imaginary friend. The truth would turn out to be altogether more profoundly sad.

As children usually do, I told my parents what I had been doing at school, which lessons I enjoyed or didn't and what my friends and I talked about. They already knew well of Susan and one or two other closer friends; Tony was a new one to them though. They wanted to know what year he was in and, I suppose with due parental care, if he might be the kind of boy their child ought to be friends with. My mother asked me to ask him about his parents, where they lived and what things Tony liked to do away from school.

I didn't see him for a few days, and then when I did I duly asked my questions and reported back his answers. He came from the same road as we lived in; he gave me the number and said he liked to ride his bike.

I remember thinking at the time how weird, as I always played out in our small cul-de-sac on my bike with all the other children from the neighbourhood and with absolute certainty I had never seen Tony there. The other thing that was odd, the number he gave me in our road belonged to an older couple and I knew for sure they had no eight-year-old boy!

I wanted to invite Tony around to our house to come and play. My parents said it wasn't really a good idea just at the moment, they would think about it later.

Our close neighbours, living two doors to the left, were an interesting couple. They had a small daughter Jo, she was around four years old and great fun, I used to play with her sometimes because her crazy antics made me laugh. Jo's parents Olive and Joe were considered a bit eccentric by most of their fellow neighbours. Olive, a psychiatric nurse, practised witchcraft and Joe, although he rarely publicly talked of it, was deeply involved in psychic research.

My mother casually invited them in for coffee and asked me to repeat all that I knew about Tony; she being a open minded enough to think I might have rather more than an imaginary friend there. Consulting the two most qualified unbiased second opinions to see what they would make of everything I had to say. Always enjoying an audience, off I went into telling my entire tale right from the beginning. Fact by fact I went through the weeks of knowing Tony and, as nobody else seemed to be able to see him, how lonely he felt most of the time.

A few years later my mother shared with me the entire conversation that took place after I left the room and the later validation of my story (more of which shortly).

At the time Joe told me that Tony sounded like he might well be a ghost and that I must be incredibly special to be able to talk with him and make friends. He explained some ghosts like to stay around in those places which meant something to them and in rare cases a ghost doesn't even know it is dead. This didn't spook me in the slightest, living where I did at that time I was all too well aware of spirits!

It simply hadn't occurred to me that Tony might actually be a ghost. I thought he must be in a different class than mine and because he didn't really mix with the other children, this is why they didn't know him. What this revelation did was make me feel sorry for Tony and I couldn't wait to see him again; as always this would be when he wanted to be seen.

I didn't have to wait too long. The sports hall at school was in that great tradition of English junior schools. With climbing ropes, an apparatus for vaulting over, exercise benches and mats, plus this climbing frame anchored against one wall. At the top of this climbing frame about three metres up sat huge window ledges, with panoramic windows overlooking the playground. As we all half reluctantly entered the hall ready for our PE lesson, Tony sat up on one of these window ledges on high, ready to watch our teacher put us through our paces. He waved at me and I winked back. He stayed there for the entire thirty-minute PE lesson, laughing sometimes at our failed attempts to carry out the simple instructions of the teacher.

I would often see Tony around school over the next few months, but by then I knew that when we finally sold the house my whole family would be moving away from the area and I would be leaving the school. Sadly I never really got the opportunity to talk properly with him again. Trying to leave Chretien Road is a story in itself which will get told in my maybe future book The Ghosts of Chretien Road.

Joe used his contacts within psychic research circles to investigate the story behind Tony based on the details I had been able to furnish him with. This is in the days before the internet; back then research meant trawling archives and old newspapers, following hunches and intuition as a guide. Piece by piece over time the tragic story began to come together.

TONY'S STORY

There had indeed been a boy called Anthony (or Tony) and as related to me by my mother when I was old enough to fully comprehend, this is the true story of Anthony …

Anthony lived in Chretien Road in the early part of the 1960's with his parents. An only child, like me all those years later, he attended the "village" school. Anthony loved to play out on his bike and he often rode the short trip to school. Part of the route to school took his mum and him alongside the busy main road into the centre of Manchester and it really was for only 25 metres (I know as I did it myself on foot every day). Horrifically he had pedalled a bit too fast, wobbled, and unable to brake in time, he left the pavement to be hit by a car and killed instantly.

THE ANGRY MAN OF CHRETIEN ROAD

I was too scared to sleep anymore...bedtime meant the terrifying ghost would make his appearance in my bedroom...as he stared at me looking so angry!

****

Bedtime had become a moment for me to dread. I knew what would happen all too soon after my head rested on my pillow. The ghost would soon make his unwanted appearance, stood right there in front of my wardrobe and looking across directly at me...

It would be a hot summer's evening the first time this ghost manifested. I went to bed at 7.30pm without fail, my mother insisted on this. On this warm evening I lay there wide awake, impatiently waiting for sleep to come, when suddenly I stared across my bedroom in sheer terror because front of the wardrobe suddenly appeared a man dressed in old fashioned clothes!

He looked straight across the room directly at me and my reaction was to immediately hide under bedcovers in the hope that he might not have noticed me and go away. Too scared to move a muscle, eventually I fell asleep. Waking in the morning I couldn't wait to tell my parents about what I witnessed the previous evening.

I went running through to the kitchen to find my mother making porridge for breakfast "I saw a man in my room last night, he stood there by my wardrobe staring at me, and I was so sacred!" My mother surprisingly wasn't as shocked to hear me tell her this this as you might expect. "Please tell me about what this man looked like" she asked "He had black hair, erm…a moustache, he stared straight at me and I was so scared!" I answered. "Do you remember anything else?" my mother asked. I replied "He looked old fashioned, you know like his clothes and he looked angry!"

My mother knew well of this apparition, for her friend Olive had told her only the day before of seeing such an apparition in her home; and from the way I described him, we undoubtedly encountered the same spirit.

Olive was invited in and we shared a conversation, with so much time elapsing I cannot recall the exact words we spoke, Olive showed me a photo in a book of Nicola Tesla and we agreed 'our' spirit shared a remarkable likeness with him. She also told me, in her opinion, 'Tesla' wasn't aware of us at all, he looked so angry because maybe he was when he died, and this is the energy he carried with him. In Olive's opinion, he was more like a robot going through the same routine on repeat, and he saw things around him as they once were for him, and I needn't be too scared as it was unlikely he even knew I was there!

I would never get to feel exactly comfortable seeing the moustachioed man in my room, and still hid beneath my covers for the time I lived in that house, however, I wasn't as scared anymore and gradually began to stop dreading bedtimes, to accept the reality of seeing a ghost in my bedroom five nights out of ten.

A THOROUGHLY UNPLEASANT SPIRIT

There stood the awful leering spirit I had felt compelled to nickname Mr Creepy as he stared at me. I sensed him deciding what he might do next…

****

In my last summer break from school at sixteen years old, I procured for myself a part-time job covering a period of two weeks. I saw it as a wonderful opportunity for some experience of the workplace for my future CV and being paid as well would certainly be appreciated. I could buy more music!

My temporary job was with the largest publishing house in Macclesfield, Cheshire. This company was based in a complex of warehouse buildings collectively known as Byron House.

Turning up for work on my first day full of enthusiasm, I reported for duty to the admin office, ready and willing to be informed of my allotted tasks.

I would be required to go down and work in the cellar. Apparently the basement of this substantial building housed a storage area or at least it had started out with the intention to be, nobody ever happened to have found the time to bring it towards its final completion and it seemed this operation now befell to me to try and make some order from the chaos.

I arrived on the day in my lovely new pinstriped suit (specially purchased for the occasion) I wanted to make a good first impression through looking serious and ready for work. I certainly hadn't anticipated I would be hanging-out in a dusty cellar!

I asked if it was okay for me to pop home to change into jeans and trainers, and they agreed to allow me as long as I didn't take too long. By the way, that would be the first and last time I would ever wear a suit to work and all in all it lasted for under half an hour!

Upon my comparatively prompt return I got met with ten humongous flat-pack boxes of industrial-strength two and a half metres high metal shelving laying there awaiting my assembly; sat adjacent to those flat-packs stood a hundred large packing cases, containing various files and the books destined for placement on the newly constructed shelves.

There I was armed with a tool-kit and vague instructions on where they required them to stand once I had erected them; admin had promptly left me on my own to simply get on with it.

Health and safety was apparently not so big in the 1980's as today. Management happy leaving an inexperienced sixteen-year-old who at that point in his life had never really held a spanner in his hand, there alone in their cellar together with approximately two tonnes worth of flat-pack metal shelving, a similar weight in boxes and absolutely no direct supervision. In fact they didn't even care to bother to venture down at any point to check on how I might be getting on or indeed if I was still alive!

Oh my, how times have certainly changed since then. Still, at least they gave me some nice yellow work gloves to protect my hands.

MEETING MR CREEPY

These cellars consisted of three substantial rooms. Two allocated for storage (my new domains) and another housing the entire boiler and heating system for the three-storey building.

Once left alone I immediately said hello to the decidedly unpleasant ghostly presence I became destined to share the cellar space with…

A male spirit dressed in a long-sleeved chequered work shirt, denim bib and braces, with receding sandy coloured hair, ruddy complexion and projecting the most repugnant energy possible to be around. It hardly surprised me that nobody lingered for too long down there!

Mr Creepy (as I rather appropriately nicknamed him) seemed to prefer the boiler room but did venture out when I loudly commenced shelf assembly and although he kept his distance, being under his leering gaze wasn't exactly the most pleasant sensation to experience. To be clear, he wasn't literally always stood manifested right there before my physical eyes, I still sensed him though and for sure I was under no doubt when he was around. He made my skin crawl standing there just staring at me, and projecting towards me his unprecedentedly nasty energy.

I did begin to feel violated and sick to my stomach by his constant predatory staring at me. I am not overstating or exaggerating when I say it felt like he was undressing me and physically assaulting me with his eyes. For sure this awful creature must have been one thoroughly disgusting man when alive, who clearly viewed young men as his prey and this ugly energy carried right on through to his spirit being.

I lasted two long days before finally admitting defeat. Going to talk with admin I politely requested some other tasks. The reason I gave was claustrophobia and to their credit they found me a nice well-lit, bright room with large windows up on the third floor...in which to assemble yet more shelves!

At sixteen years old I had much yet to learn about life and of the paranormal. Although by then ghosts failed to deeply scare or move me too much, I did find co-existing with entities such as Mr Creepy a definite challenge. Nowadays I would be completely hands-on and deal with him accordingly to cleanse the space. And in his particular case I would truly enjoy doing so!

ATTACKED BY SPIRITS!

The maelstrom of paranormal activity raged all around me. Getting more extreme and off the scale by the minute. Then the screaming noise of the fire alarm piercingly assaulted my ears once more. I found myself wondering what exactly these spirits would do to me if I didn't get out of this building and fast...

****

Oak House had already stood for one hundred and fifty years. Once a neo-Georgian three-storey townhouse, it got converted some years ago into offices. Still retaining many original features, such as the beautifully panelled doors, ornate corniced ceilings, and marble fireplaces; it certainly made for one interesting place to work.

A labyrinth of corridors and staircases leant atmosphere, adding to the sense of stepping back in time within the building. It remained consistently a similar temperature as you entered Oak House via the impressive red mosaic tiled entrance hall, come summer or winter it ranged from coolish to sometimes genuinely freezing cold.

Here was a building which, although altered through the years to become offices, retained the ambience of a bygone age. Perhaps to do with the fixtures and fittings, yet also it didn't take too much of a leap of imagination to vision how it might once have looked and functioned as someone's home. Overlooking the ancient market area of Macclesfield, Cheshire in England, it must have stood out as a splendid residence in the early through to mid twentieth century.

I began working in Oak House at around twenty after college, within two years becoming the sole in-house graphic designer. I was already quite experienced in matters of the paranormal, although considerably less hands-on with any activity I encountered at this earlier point in my development. My more interactive approach would arrive later. Definitely as fully aware as I am now, I nevertheless hadn't quite yet matured into my full potential.

Oak House was what most only be described as this veritable hub of paranormal encounters and spirit activity!

Even my once more sceptical colleagues had inevitably been forced to come around to accepting we certainly shared our offices with many mostly (but certainly not always) unseen occupants. Items they were using for their work would mysteriously disappear from where they usually belonged, only to reappear sometime later exactly where they ought to be. Reports came of shadow figures seen out on the stairs and often in one particular office footsteps heard, yet nobody to be seen. In fact, all of the generally accepted disturbances associated with a seriously haunted building!

Dowsing was now part of my life and having used my pendulum in Oak House I was able to confirm (as if it actually needed any confirming!) here we all collectively worked alongside many unseen dwellers within the building.

My graphic design studio was located right up on the top floor of the building. A large open room covering the entire front of the building, natural light afforded by panoramic windows all along one wall, with views out over the hustle and bustle of the main street and marketplace. Yet alone up there, overlooking everything from so far above, I always did feel myself a little remote from the happenings of the outside world.

I was indeed alone for most of my working day and I usually found myself the only occupant on this level of the building. The rest of the top floor offices were only used for storage or vacant entirely. My huge studio must have originally been two large bedrooms and extremely impressive they would have looked.

The nature of my work meant sometimes there was only a little to do and other times it all got quite intense, more than once necessitating me working all-night shifts to get design jobs off to print the following morning. It worked for everyone that I worked more flexible hours. I was also studying body language psychology part-time and this job allowed me the luxury of easily being able to fit this in. All in all then a perfect win/win for everyone.

On these all-night sessions I rarely got the sense of much in the way of the paranormal, yes okay occasionally I felt I was getting watched as I slogged onwards until the rising dawn to see yet another design job through to completion. By and large though the spirits seemed to respect my space enough to simply let me get on with what I needed to do.

My colleagues were never too keen to visit me up there on the top floor. A large wide well-lit staircase led up to my level and then turning left into a darkly narrow annex off, is where my studio door stood. I suppose it must have felt claustrophobic approaching the studio, once inside though it was an entirely different matter as the large bright space assaulted suddenly overwhelmed eyes. Co-workers seldom stayed up there for too long and I don't care to think it could have been down to my company or choice of music (I would often play and sing along as best I could to Italian opera or enjoy some other classical music on the radio while I worked). They all stated they were ill at ease walking the gloomy annex into my studio and couldn't wait to get back down to the main office on the first floor!

I had been impatiently waiting since Thursday for a courier to deliver some missing information and then I would at last be able to finish off the design job I had been halfway through. Finally, late on Friday afternoon, the missing piece of the puzzle arrived and the usual hive of activity ensued to sign-off another project completed. Working late wasn't an option this particular Friday, I did have a social life as well as my work and so needing only an hour or thereabouts left to finish off the job, away I went at 5pm to get ready for an evening out with my girlfriend.

I had the idea to come into the office for an hour on Saturday morning, long enough to complete the project, leaving Monday then free to start afresh on something else. As I knew I needed to come into town anyway, it all seemed like the perfect solution.

ARRIVAL

Parking in my usual place on the otherwise deserted office car park, I made my way to the front door of Oak House. Literally as I put my passkey into the lock I heard the fire alarm suddenly shriek into life.

Fortunately the alarm control panel happened to be located right by the entrance to the building, just to the left inside the front door. Sensors were positioned all throughout the building, warning of fire and setting off the central alarm. According to the read-out on this control panel the apparent fire was on the top level, right there outside the door to my studio!

Turning off the volume I cautiously proceeded up the two levels of rather uneven stairs as quickly as I was able while nursing a hangover and wearing cowboy boots that with hindsight weren't the wisest choice of footwear on the day, but I wasn't to know when getting ready to go out in the morning exactly what kind of weirdness would unfold for me on that Saturday. Once upstairs I thoroughly checked to see if the building was indeed ablaze. Thankfully no actual fire having been discovered raging outside my studio door or anywhere else close by and no tell-tale smell of smoke, I decided I would report an obviously faulty sensor to management first thing on Monday morning.

Putting it all out of my mind, I unlocked the studio door and turned on all my equipment to warm-up ready for the task ahead. In an instant everything suddenly felt extremely wrong. Dark oppressive energy surrounded me, which I confess took me completely off guard. I started in surprise, which if you have been reading these adventures so far you will know me well enough to agree is unlike my usual reaction when dealing with the paranormal. Then the hairs on my arms prickled; classic signs of something paranormal occurring. For sure, this was going to be weird, even by my standards.

As this was a sunny autumn day I opened a window and pulled up the blinds to let more natural light in. Then everything started getting even crazier. I got this strong sense of multiple spirits wanting me out of the building. Well okay, that's one massive understatement! I could feel they absolutely hated me with a burning passion and my presence at that particular Saturday!!!

And then it happened again. Shriek! The fire alarm cut through the silence. It felt like pushing against a thick psychic soup getting down the stairs to disable it. This time the sensor on the first floor set it off, the same one I just passed seconds ago on my way down to the ground floor. I disabled the alarm once more.

Next I carefully and deliberately walked up to the main first floor office to unlock the door, my senses never more overloaded! The main printer was located there and as I knew I would need it at some point, reaching behind I plugged it into the electrical socket ready. To the right of the printer a large colourful hardboard poster of a jungle scene (complete with tiger) had been pinned to the wall above the fireplace in this room. As I was turning on the printer, this heavy poster leapt straight off the wall, hitting me a glancing blow on my right arm on its way to the floor, which hurt quite a lot and left a large purple bruise. It had been attached to the wall by around ten 3cm panel pins and I cannot imagine there being any chance it might possibly have simply fallen off the wall, plus I was stood partially to the right of its trajectory in the unlikely event it had. Yet this poster somehow managed to fall in my direction to hit my arm, rather than drop straight onto the floor in front of the fireplace.

DEPARTURE

I resolved there and then to leave the building at my earliest opportunity. First though I would have to turn off all my equipment upstairs and that meant a journey back up to the top floor studio. Knocks and crashes were coming from out on the stairway, yet there in the main office spirits had made it obvious beyond any doubt I wasn't welcome, I knew staying there was not an option.

I left the first-floor main office, making sure I locked the door and breathed deeply to remain calm. Bang, bang, bang! The sound of multiple footsteps right behind and around me on the stairs. I don't generally panic given exposure to the paranormal; here though I knew the spirits would go to any extreme lengths to get me out of the building as they had already physically hurt me!

Talking out loud I told them I was going to leave. I said I respected their right to have the space to themselves today and didn't wish to get in their way. I half-jokingly further said if they wanted to invite their ghostly friends from all across the neighbourhood around for a party this Saturday that was fine by me and I was more than willing to leave them in peace. Perhaps there could have been more truth in my joke than I gave credit to at the time. I have visited a multitude of highly paranormal locations in my life and never experienced so many spirits gathered in one place all at one time as on that particular Saturday. The vast number of spirits rendered it impossible for any kind of one-on-one communication. My only option became on that day to take my leave of Oak House and let the spirits get on with whatever their purpose might be.

Slowly I made my way up to my studio; feeling pressed upon from all sides and yet determined to remain calm. What awaited me chilled me through to my soul.

My radio played out at full volume into the room!!!

I knew with absolute certainty I had not turned it on, as I mentioned earlier I was suffering from a headache as an after effect from my socializing the night before and I made the conscious decision that I wanted quiet while I worked. Furthermore, the blinds I earlier opened were now drawn shut and the windows all closed…

Methodically I turned the radio off and did the same with the rest of my equipment. Leaving the room and locking my door behind me to descend the stairs to the ground floor. I don't remember too much of the descent other than an overwhelming sense of threat and (even in those days, as now, I did as a matter of course use a lot of psychic self-defence) the sense that anything might happen, which would certainly be entirely outside of my control. Finally reaching the ground floor one final shocking event was about to play out…

On my way to escape through the exit door, as I passed by the control panel for the fire alarm, the high decibel siren screamed into life once more. Checking the readout confirmed the sensor which had been triggered this time. And it was the very one on the ceiling not more than a metre right there above my own head exactly where I was stood! Quickly rebooting the system, I got out of the place and didn't look back.

Standing outside in the sun, as the door self-locked, looking around I saw shoppers going about their usual weekend routine, making the whole experience seem even more bizarre and surreal. That I would find myself interacting with spirits came as no great surprise to me, after all I had been aware of their existence since I was a little boy, and yet effectively being thrown out onto the street from my place of work by ghosts was definitely a new one even for me!

I chose not to mention my ghostly experience to any of my colleagues, they already teased me about my lack of vices and love of crystals, calling me by the nick-name which has followed me around since college, namely Saint.

Monday morning though did find some direct evidence left of what occurred two days before, not least the poster in the main office laying on the floor and chairs not quite where they usually were. The clearest evidence I got, and again I kept this to myself, existed as a large, booted footprint right across the middle of one of a group of A4 sized black and white photographs I had been sorting through on the floor. My door was always kept locked and no other members of staff had access to the studio, apart from the managing director and even if he had somehow failed to see the large collection of over-sized photos spread right across the floor to inadvertently step on one, he always wore business shoes and not the riding boot it would seem had left their imprint.

I did dutifully report the fire alarm might have been malfunctioning. The engineer came the same day and tested the entire system. Naturally he found it all worked perfectly and gave it a clean bill of health.

Later on Monday, taking a quiet moment to psychically reach out into the ethers of the building and the spirits, everything seemed to be back to as normal as it ever was likely to be. I dowsed to confirm my intuitive feelings to get a positive response of Yes, everything had settled back into the usual equilibrium.

Shortly after this experience, but certainly not because of it, I left to start my own business, which took me off to another part of the country for a short while.

GHOSTS WITH NO PLACE TO CALL HOME

As the wrecking ball moved in he cried out for help!

****

Spirits who choose to stay around partially on the physical plane are usually strongly connected to a particular location. Such a place existed in my former hometown of Macclesfield, Cheshire. Well to be more accurate, an infinite number of haunted places existed in that town. With its strong industrial history, it is hardly surprising countless restless souls, who perhaps passed far before their time, felt compelled to stay close to those areas they lived or worked in. Although for this story, the ghostly tale centres on only the one location.

This building, although I never personally investigated it, for sure had its resident spirit entity. I felt his presence every single time I passed on by. And as is my way, I usually said hello as I elegantly sauntered my way past the wonderfully decaying front door.

I have absolutely no idea for how long this building had lain empty, for sure in all the period I had up to that point resided in the town, it slowly but surely gently had become more charismatically distressed as the years passed on by and its unseen occupant went undisturbed.

Change happened, as it is often prone to do and presently a demolition crew moved into the area. I love to record in photographs older parts of towns and cities. How often I have found upon subsequent revisits these splendid old buildings to have gone, making way for what is apparently considered progress. I often think how wonderful it would be to rescue these fast-disappearing relics of a bygone time, rather in the manner of Clough Williams-Ellis and his visionary Portmeirion in Wales.

Upon standing taking what would become a series of photographs of Macclesfield caught in the process of turbulent redevelopment, I sensed multiple spirits equally in turmoil. The locations they had for so long enjoyed such an inseparable connection with, now fast disappearing under an ungainly pile of demolition rubble.

It does happen more frequently these days that I find myself called into nearly new buildings to ostensibly clear a ghost or some other kind of manifestation. The client usually mystified, with the smell of new plaster and paint still fresh in their building, how they might possibly have ended up sharing their space with such an unwanted lodger. A little research and dowsing generally confirms the existence of previous buildings in precisely the same location to which theirs now stands; a spirit is then simply carrying on with business as usual, despite the hotspot they were connected to literally no longer physically being there any more.

Other times such radical change forcefully cleanses the spirit entity from the location completely.

In the case of the building in question I took several photos during various stages of its destruction. Connecting briefly to the spirit entity now experiencing complete bewilderment during one of my earlier visits, I sent the suggestion the time had finally come for him to move on...

More recently revisiting this area in Macclesfield of my earlier photographic expedition, I must admit myself deeply saddened to realise all those fine old buildings had gone to make way for just a car park!

WAS NICOLAS POSSESSED?

The strange news had reached me, unusual and arcane things have a habit of doing. Nicolas had fallen to the floor in the process of choking while waving away all offers of assistance...as his invisible assailant continued in its relentless attack...

****

Nicolas was and is an extremely private person. Sharing with others anything he might personally feel afflicted with is never easy for Nicolas. His priority is helping others, usually placing his own needs last. His personal passion was and is helping the homeless in whatever way he can. I knew him already through the homeless shelter we both volunteered at.

For some two months he had been experiencing what felt like a constriction in his throat, he said to him it felt like some unseen entity was in the process of gently attempting to throttle him!

He did his best to ignore what he tried to persuade himself to be only a slight inconvenience, doing his level best to continue with life as usual.

I knew I might afford a complete healing for Nicolas, if only given the opportunity. He simply needed to request my help, otherwise I could do nothing. The trouble is I think he found me a bit intimidating to be honest. Nicolas is a small slightly-built man and I am quite tall. In my back-then typical cowboy boots I towered over him at around six foot three or 190cm, poor little Nicolas actually didn't even reach up to my shoulders in height! Nicolas was (and is) a no-nonsense practical kind of man. With the crystals and magical amulets I wore back then, in combination with my gypsy sense of fashion, looking like a long lost member of Dexy's Midnight Runners; and the fact I also tended to talk in slightly over-the-top positive philosophy cliches pretty much all the time; I imagine to Nicolas I was just simply too far-out weird for his taste! He did confide in me later he felt sure I was some kind of sorcerer or wizard (guilty as charged!).

I do still possess a positive mindset; the difference is that these days though I prefer to let my actions speak for themselves and will only share my inner philosophy with those who ask me about it.

After personally witnessing one of his choking episodes and quite obviously not being in the slightest bit phased by what played out before me, finally led Nicolas to shyly ask me what I thought might be happening to him and as he blushed further, rather reluctantly request if I might be able to help him…

I had a fairly good idea what Nicolas's issue might be. As usual when offering any healing I told him I could offer no guarantees regarding results, nevertheless promised some distant healing on his behalf. In front of him I immediately consulted my pendulum to establish beyond doubt the exact location of his emotional blockage, and further asked out loud the question "can I help Nicolas?" to happily get my Yes response. To be honest this question was more for the benefit of Nicolas, as I already knew I could help!

Dowsing in private later confirmed my suspicions as to what Nicolas found himself having to contend with. His case wasn't that unusual in my experience. I instinctively sensed why he had an emotional blockage, using my pendulum validated my initial intuitive feeling. This blockage affected him physically and would only intensify if left unchecked. Quite commonplace in those who seek me out kind of help, I generally deal with them comparatively easily.

Nicolas possessed a strong emotional blockage in his throat chakra and ultimately it took me three distant healing sessions to totally understand all the nuances behind it. In his case this blockage had gradually built up over a period of over a year because of unexpressed feelings of frustration and powerlessness, buried deep inside of him and never allowed the opportunity to be verbally expressed, which of course would have allowed him to subsequently heal. This had physically manifested as his throat issues and the all too real feeling of choking. This throat chakra blockage developed due to him feeling unable to communicate his inner feelings to anyone.

Having once worked in senior management within local government, due to downsizing his department, Nicolas found himself unexpectedly made redundant slightly over a year before. I suggested to Nicolas his need to heal himself through finally confronting this traumatic situation from a year ago, the one he never dealt with or talked about to anyone. I explained to him that in order to practically be able continue in his self-confessed quest to assist others, he needed to firstly help himself by letting go of his past career and his self-image which went with it. This became practically essential in order to move on with his life.

He talked with me for several hours about all his sense of loss as his much-loved career ended and lacking any real motivation to start all over again.

Deep down though he knew he had grieved for his past-life for long enough. He equally sensed it was high time to find something new to excite his interest. After this conversation, dowsing confirmed his issue dealt with...

Finally cleared of his emotional blockage, Nicolas knew he needed purpose to his life once more and to live taking due care of his own wellbeing. If he existed in a happy and healthy state, he would find it far easier to help others.

He commenced sincerely seeking a new direction from life and in due course opportunity came along for him to work within an exciting career close not only his own front door, but definitely even more close to his heart. Nicolas found his ideal employment managing the same shelter for the homeless we had both previously been volunteering at for the last year!

GHOST HIKERS?

It took a moment to register with me such was my surprise at the apparent reality of what had just occurred. As I often did in those days, I had walked all day in the Derbyshire Peak District. In the twilight of this late summer's day I had just been wished "Guten Morgen" by the couple passing by me in the opposite direction...

****

I lived in a cute unmodernised period cottage with an extensive wild rear garden, which is what sold it to me. Located just outside of Macclesfield right on the edge of the Derbyshire Peak District and furthermore having a love of hill walking, I had right there at my disposal one of the more beautiful areas of the United Kingdom. All I needed to do was turn right from out of my front door and within half an hour urban civilization had been left far behind.

The only downside, living as I did in the valley, every walking adventure first required a test of stamina due to the steeply uphill pathway leading for over two miles to The Peak District, although philosophically I considered the ascent at least allowed me to enjoy the easier descent back home after a day's exploring. I am especially fond of this first home of mine as this is where I started my writing career with the original edition of Anyone Can Dowse.

This beautiful warm day in August found me donning my lightweight summer walking gear and heading out on one such adventure. Having set out at around 9am, everything I needed for the day was safely stored away in my bag, travelling light just the way I liked it. My trail took me through the heady scents of Macclesfield Forest. This area has its own stories to tell, there are many mysterious buildings dotted around the forest in various states of ruin, and for sure they are mostly haunted!

From the forest I walked over gorsy moorland and eventually down into my favourite area, known as the Goyt Valley.

My first stop as always came when I arrived at the Goyt Valley Shrine, a cute petite building rather resembling a mustard pot. The Shrine was constructed in the nineteenth century in lasting remembrance of a much-loved children's governess who died comparatively young, hailing from the now dismantled Errwood Hall, further along the valley. At some point I will write of my own experiences at the Errwood Hall site, but that is also a story for another book at another time.

Passing through the low doorway to find the tiny interior, as usual, bedecked with flowers. I so often wondered who ensured there were continuously fresh flowers left in there. The paranormal presence felt gentle and tranquil, I cannot be sure if indeed she is the actual governess, but certainly a female spirit for sure. I left her in the same peace as she brings to all those who care to visit the shrine.

Back out into the heat of the midday sun, with my lunch consumed, adventure resumed. Much later that day saw me making another stop to admire the scenery and eating the rest of my snacks, checking the time to see it was now shortly past 6pm. My cue to start heading back…

Another long uphill trek taking me out of the Goyt Valley could be put off no longer. Suitably sustained onwards I strode. Eventually finding myself feeling tiny out on the vast wide-open moorland and with a promise to myself of a stop-off at the Cat and Fiddle Inn for a taste or two of their finest organic ales.

UNEXPLAINABLE ENCOUNTER

With my attention focussed on the welcoming ale awaiting me, I half registered a young couple walking towards me down the pathway. Dressed in shorts, walking boots and with back-packs I took them to be simply fellow hillwalkers on their way back to the car park I passed some mile or so back down in the valley.

"Guten Morgen!" they both cheerfully proclaimed as they passed on by me. As I smiled back in response, suddenly the unlikeness of what had just occurred struck me. As I felt static passing over my body, causing goose-bumps, I knew I had just experienced paranormal activity!

Determined to talk further with this couple, moments later I turned intending to retrace my steps to catch them up.

To be greeted by an empty moor!

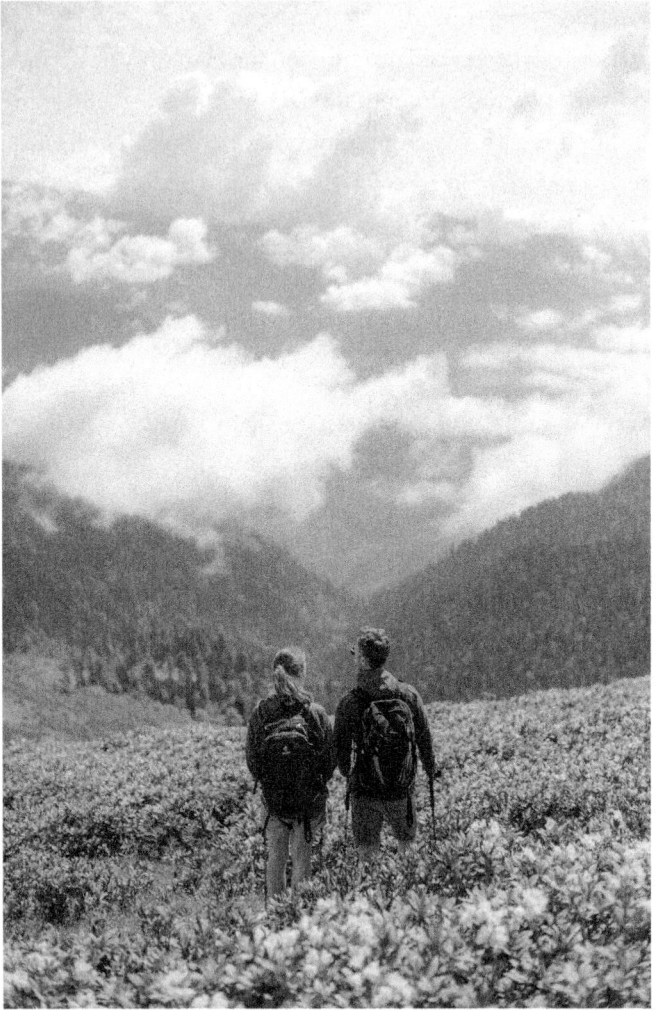

Not a single solitary person in my line of sight for as far as I could see, for sure plenty of sheep, but certainly no humans. I need to emphasize and stress there were quite literally no possible places anyone could have hidden out of sight! No walls or trees, no valleys, and no roads they might have been picked up by a passing car from. Only vast open moorland, completely empty apart from many sheep and me!

I ran, suddenly my end-of-day aches forgotten, rapidly retracing my steps back down towards the Goyt Valley. Eventually reaching the plateau from where it is possible to see right down the path all the way back to the car park.

No trace of anyone to be seen…

I should also stress there existed absolutely no other direction this couple could have taken. Diverting away from the footpath out onto the wild open moor was largely impossible due to the thick gorse, and anyway even if they had somehow managed to continue walking in any other direction for sure I would have easily seen them.

And then something else struck me, chilling me right through despite the still pleasantly warm evening sun. I assumed when they had passed me by they would be making their way to the car park marking the end of the footpath, and yet when I walked through the same car park less than an hour before it had lain completely empty, then as now there were no cars parked there. Furthermore, if a car had travelled from out of the valley I would have certainly heard as it laboured up the steep road, the sound easily carrying all the way over to the footpath I was on.

Searching everywhere for nearly two hours and no trace could be found of my fellow hill-walkers. Even though I knew for certain there could not have been anywhere else they might have ventured away from the designated footpath, as always, I wanted to be sure to investigate what I had witnessed in an attempt to debunk it.

As Conan Doyle's world-famous fictional Victorian detective regularly observed, having eliminated every rational possibility, explored any other improbable explanation, there is only one possible logical conclusion I can reach. On that day, for whatever arcane reason and only the goddess will understand why, I interacted with a couple of German speaking ghost hikers…

FAE HOUSE-SHARE

The fairy dwellers I encountered in my garden felt it was high-time they moved into my cottage with me...

****

I consider myself fortunate and indeed blessed to be able to see a little of what lays beyond our third dimensional world.

And such it was I found myself fascinated by the fae folk I encountered in the extensive wild garden area to the rear of my first home. Please be aware I wasn't literally stood there staring at them manifested gloriously in full sight before me. I caught glimpses of them and over time became conversant enough with their appearance to offer you a full description of how they looked.

Approximately two foot in height, walking (rather than being airborne) and they wore knee-length hooded coats. These coats were in different shades of nature, specific to each of these individual natural entities, some were green, others brown or orange and then there were a few also in mid-blue. As their hoods were up I couldn't see their hair colour, but they had for want of a better description, somewhat puckish faces.

Fae folk live a kind of life totally alien to us. A different code of ethics, and despite their deep connection to nature, they are not always automatically benevolent in their attitude towards humans. They can bestow favours upon us should the mood take them, however, if they feel due respect for their ways and lore is not observed they can be at the very least mischievous or sometimes rarely even downright unpleasant.

Having experienced countless encounters with every variety of faerie, natural elemental and on one occasion an actual Green Man (stories to be shared in some future book) I find it consistently fascinating to know there are an infinite number more mysteries I have yet to discover. Indeed, even those fae folk I have witnessed or even managed to directly interact with still keep some of their secrets tantalizingly to themselves.

These fae people lived in nature outside my home for more than likely well before it had ever got built; and for a while they seemed quite happy to remain outside.

That is until one night when, leaving the bedroom to visit the bathroom in the early hours of the morning I vividly saw them milling all around me in the hallway!

I must confess to total surprise at finding these faeries inside my home; for sure I knew they were aware of me; and especially me being able to see them. Indeed I often talked to them while out in my lovely wild garden, and I believe this is where I made this fundamental error of judgement. Communicating with them more or less as friends while enjoying sitting out in the sun reading a book or when attempting to tame my garden at least a bit, I suppose they felt within their lore that I had invited them to share my home. I also talked to the birds, hedgehogs and moles out in my garden but thankfully they didn't move in with me as well!

Unwilling to banish them (I would never be as foolish as to offend fae folk!) for the time we lived there we both got more used to playing host to our sometimes daytime and yet more often nocturnal guests. Showing them our due respect and expecting exactly the same in return.

SEEING THE LIGHTS

As we had two lounges in our home, I converted the front room into a meeting room; originally intending it to be used for giving consultations to smaller groups of people, although it never really ended up being used for this purpose. In there I managed to capture a photo of what I believe is the fae folk manifested as light phenomena. Nothing appeared visible to the naked eye when I took this.

Often orbs or blobs of light are the most witnessed of paranormal activity. Other types of light manifestation also occur, and these range from larger light shapes, through to virtually rooms full of lights, white smoke or the classic darker shadow images.

It seems my own personal light manifestation calling card is electric blue light. Those individuals I practice distant psychic healing for frequently talk of witnessing blue sparks (rather like LED lights) in their vicinity as the session is underway. Beforehand they are generally unaware of the precise moment I am offering the healing, afterwards their feedback and reports of the blue sparks coincides with the corresponding time I worked in my particular manner on their behalf.

Rarely does it happen that it is possible to find an image of fae folk captured in plain sight within a photograph. In over two decades of keen photography, having taken many thousands of images, I have only managed to record fae folk less than a dozen or so times.

If you ever find yourself fortunate enough to encounter faerie folk be sure to treat them with respect, they are deeply connected to our eco-system and feel extremely protective of nature...

CARS AND GHOSTS

When not dealing with the ghostly and paranormal, I enjoy playing with classic cars. Oftentimes I feel during more complex engineering challenges it might be useful to have some help. In a sense my wish came true when a man in blue engineer's overalls commenced observing me from a few metres away...

****

Giving talks and my burgeoning writing career had taken precedence in my life for a while. Eventually and inevitably paranormal investigation cases soon started to become the focus of my attention once more.

At that time I resided in a tiny village with a population of only a few hundred people. Located in Derbyshire, my personal favourite part of this home had to be the outside. Parking area extensive enough for many cars to easily fit; and even better than that, a rather wonderful double garage with an inspection pit built in.

Although my motor engineering knowledge is far from extensive, I enjoyed the challenge of working on my latest project, and I spent many happy hours tinkering with this car, a classic Mini, in my double garage.

Determined it would be roadworthy soon, on this spring day I lifted it up on ramps and having carefully climbed underneath into the pit, I occupied myself dealing with inspecting the exhaust system that needed repairing, when looking out onto the driveway through the open door I saw a pair of feet!

Clad in heavy brown work-boots, these feet belonged to the lower leg parts of blue overalls, and this was as far as I was able to see from my position. Stationed about three or four metres away, from the direction the feet were facing, clearly whoever owned them was engaged in watching me. Gently easing my way up the ladder out of the pit, fully with the intention of greeting my uninvited visitor, slowly emerging I discovered there to be nobody there. No feet and equally definitely no person.

Surprisingly given my particular field of expertise it simply didn't even cross my mind I might be witnessing anything in the slightest bit paranormal here. I can only surmise with my thoughts being so preoccupied with the practical work I was involved with, I imagined blue overall man must have simply run off seeing me getting up, thinking I was about to scold him for being on my property.

I have always ensured I have a den for myself in all the homes where I have lived. In my den at this place there was a large window overlooking the drive leading to the garage. The next day saw me relaxing reading a book in my den. I happened to glance up out of the window and there on the driveway stood my engineering friend once again.

And now it all made sense!

Feeling slightly embarrassed about the first time I saw him failing to recognise a spirit when I witnessed one and my erroneous conclusion. There is oftentimes the incorrect assumption ghosts must be shadow figures or in some way transparent. And while this sometimes is indeed how they manifest; it certainly doesn't always work out quite that way.

Blue overall man looked to be about sixty years old. He had dark brown going to grey curly hair, of average in height and a few days of stubble on his chin.

The impression he gave was of the archetypal garage mechanic or motor engineer and in his manifestation he was solid enough for me to be able to see the oil stains on his overalls and dirty hands more or less the size of small shovels!

Immediately I set off to the garage, seeing if I would be able to establish contact. Taking maybe twenty seconds to reach the exact spot he had stood moments before. I called him out, reaching towards him. We made contact and he said that he wanted to be called Henry, although

I am absolutely positive this was not his real name and I am equally positive he knew I was fully aware of this. Anyway, Henry he wanted, so Henry I called him.

Not being entirely sure at the time what his reasons were for the alias, looking back though, perhaps he simply didn't wish to be traced through his previous human life, happy to remain a bit of a mystery. Henry had actually been a farmer, not a mechanic; nevertheless he possessed extensive knowledge of all things mechanical. The over-riding vibe I got from him was that here I had contacted a thoroughly pleasant man, in no way threatening and equally quite happy to remain where he was. Henry had no desire to be shown the light.

Work continued with my classic car project as long as my other work allowed. I enjoyed having Henry around and I cannot say for definite, but I am as sure as I can be that those particularly tricky bits I struggled with I got a little extra encouragement and instruction.

I stayed in that village under two years. My truth about the paranormal is there are either positive and negative ghosts or entities, just as there are with people. And I do like to think that Henry and I would have been good friends had we physically met a few years before (then again, perhaps we were really great friends anyway...)

I enjoyed working on the car. I eventually got it finished that summer with a little help from Henry and an awful lot more from my local garage and this same garage bought it off me in the end.

I think I will share two out of sequence car-related stories to end this chapter because I sense you will enjoy them; and then get back on track to our timeline once more for the next chapter.

A HAUNTED TOYOTA

As you may have deduced my life frequently consists of weird and bizarre experiences. Although I do also have some mundanely ordinary days as well though where I go give a talk somewhere, drive home to eat my evening meal and wash my clothes (honestly!). One of the more unusual experiences though for sure would definitely be finding myself in possession of a possessed car!

This particular Toyota Corolla attracted me as I am always interested in any classic cars and here this one offered a winning combination of extremely low miles and it looked pretty much showroom fresh. This Toyota proved irresistible to me, it simply had to be mine!

All was good upon collecting it on the allotted day and to drive the experience confirmed it did feel much like a new car. Researching a little of its history I discovered it to have had only one previous elderly gentleman owner since new and for some reason his daughter had sold on his car to the garage I later purchased it from. It didn't take too much of a leap of imagination to conclude why exactly that might have been the case.

The previous owner seriously liked his car, he kept it immaculately clean, each and every maintenance receipt logged and filed in date order. So much was the level if his attachment to his Toyota that he even started to accompany me on journeys! Sensing him sat right beside me in the passenger seat or if travelling with my partner Kiki, he sat in the back seat there behind us.

Action needed to be taken by me. I didn't have anything especially against Ernest personally, but felt as my name was on the documents as the registered owner, spirit or not it had for sure become time for him to let go!

In the nicest, gentlest possible way I exorcised him from my Toyota. Not from the connections to his family he clearly wished to remain around for now, just from out of my car.

ELLE

For the last few years I've been the proud owner of my 2CV called Elle (after the way the number plate looks). I adore and love this little car so much I intend to keep her forever, presuming fossil fuel cars don't become totally obsolete. And should they, then I'm just going to have to have her converted to electric power. That's how much I love my cutey-car!

After ten years of poor health, in 2019 my mother passed away from multiple heath issues. Sadly she never got to travel in Elle, she enjoyed going places with me, but she didn't get the opportunity of taking any journeys with me in this car.

Elle lives in the driveway to our cottage when she is asleep; one day Kiki told me to come quickly as my mother, who had passed only a few weeks previously, was sat right there in the passenger seat of my car on the driveway! We both stood at the window to quite clearly see her right there for a minute, before she slowly faded away...

As you might have gathered by now I don't really leave ghostly encounters just at that, even regardless of this manifestation apparently being my own mother, I still needed to investigate a little further to see why.

When the house was quiet, with Kiki staying away a for few days for her work, I reached out to my mother to see what I sensed. I got she regretted never getting to go anywhere with me in Elle; I promised we would put that right and go to our favourite place the next day, which happened to fall on a weekend and I already knew I had no other pressing commitments.

I set off early driving to the Welsh Coast the following morning, I immediately sensed her presence beside me, I could smell the unique fragrance of her home-blended perfume. I drove to our special place, went for a longish walk and later returned home in mid afternoon.

Although when getting out of bed in the mornings I do still occasionaly hear her voice out loud saying "hello darling" to me, she never repeated her manifestation in my car. I do still love to visit our special place though and feel closer to her there...

WHAT GHOST?

"I am too scared to stay alone in my own house!" Sandra declared. Promising a full-on paranormal investigation reassured her "Thank you babe! Otherwise I'll have to move, I can't sleep properly here any more!"

****

Investigating cases occasionally sees me looking past the apparent concrete evidence to dig down far deeper to uncover the less obvious story which often exists just beyond the evidence.

Sandra was a friend of Kiki's and I; and one such event where I needed to look far beyond claims of paranormal activity is when Sandra insisted her rented house in the Midlands area of England to be profoundly haunted. Although having spent some time there, I confessed to experiencing none of my usual reactions to paranormal activity, I nevertheless promised her I would undertake a thorough investigation.

Asking to be left there on my own overnight, off Sandra cooperatively went without any persuasion to spend the stormy winter's night with her sister and quite happily left me to see what I would see.

Early evening commenced with initially gentle bangs, followed by loud thumping noises cutting through the silence. Following the source of these dramatic sounds confirmed my suspicions. Having subsequently bled the excess air out of the central heating radiators throughout the property, these intrusive noises ceased.

The next strange phenomenon occurred one hour later, as I witnessed before my eyes the kitchen door leading into the dining room close entirely of its own accord!

Investigating led me to the kitchen extractor fan, which had become lodged in a permanently open position. After a little penetrating oil and to gently easing it back and forth until free to function as intended, the draught on this windy evening causing the door to slam closed apparently spontaneously was also eradicated.

One of those occasions where I am compelled to put aside psychic investigation to take on a different role as a maintenance engineer, in this case all that became necessary was a little lateral thought to cleanse the house of all its unwelcome distractions.

Debunking often occurs during the course of a case, I never mind, ensuring clients feel comfortable within their environment are clearly of paramount importance. Regardless of the investigation giving evidence of a genuine haunting or as in this case something altogether more mundane it hardly matters; the important point is getting to the heart of the issue, whatever it actually may be and dealing with it in the most appropriate way.

A DRAMATIC CHANGE OF LIFESTYLE NEEDED!

As I dowsed to get to the heart of her issue it became apparent Eleanor needed to change her lifestyle and like now…otherwise she would soon become seriously ill…

****

Most of my healing for others these days is done over a distance, this way I get to help so many more people, the majority of who I usually never get to physically meet. This case was just such an occasion. Eleanor wasn't just in another country from where I am based; she was on a different continent, located on more or less the other side of the world from me in New Zealand.

The email which arrived one particular day once again confirmed to me one truth which has been proved right countless times - there are some people who remain destined to cross our paths for a pre-determined reason, even if initially we have practically no idea what this reason might be!

The woman in question getting in touch was definitely a serendipitous happening. Her email enquired if I might help her, after me asking exactly how, Eleanor took the opportunity to tell me all her story. Sharing innermost feelings for the first time which she knew those close around her would find a too odd to fully understand.

Her reality was she felt unhappy, lacking energy and much motivation to change anything in her life – whilst paradoxically knowing deep down inside her that she definitely needed to do precisely that. She felt lethargic, was overweight and her underlying fear was she could have some serious illness all the health professionals had missed during her frequent visits for consultation.

Promising I would dowse to investigate further for her, here I found myself presented with an opportunity to stretch my own ability to the outer limits. To afford a healing session for someone who not only lived on the opposite side of the globe, but in a completely different time-zone; I must confess I found myself fascinated to see how it might all work out for both of us!

Getting out my dowsing pendulum to consult, as usual allowed me to get straight to the heart of the matter for Eleanor. When we don't actually have our client right there in front of us to ask pertinent questions or watch their body language as they respond, our pendulum proves invaluable.

These are the questions I asked relating to this case:

1. Has Eleanor got some as yet undiagnosed illness? (answer Maybe)

2. Does Eleanor have emotional blockages? (No)

3. One emotional blockage? (No)

4. Multi-layered emotional blockages? (No)

5. Are my intuitive senses of what is causing these issues for Eleanor correct? (Yes)

6. Will a healing session from here be able to help Eleanor? (Yes)

Using a piece of quartz crystal as a magnifier of my energy, I commenced with my distant healing session, more this time to get a sense of exactly how I might help Eleanor and what was literally her issue.

Please understand, when one such as myself does a distant healing we cannot read the client's mind, all their personal and private thoughts remain just that, private. What I did feel strongly coming back from Eleanor was her physical body crying-out in distress. The strongest sense she needed to change her eating habits and like now!

I am not a qualified nutritionist, what I do have though, as a plant-based eater, is three decades of experience in being vigilant in what I choose to take into my body by way of food and drink.

Getting it touch with her again, Eleanor confirmed back by email that, although she was vegetarian, her diet consisted mainly of microwaved convenience fast-food and the only liquid she took on board all day were soda and energy drinks. Little wonder she experienced mood swings and stamina issues!

My urgent suggestion to Eleanor was she needed to reduce her sugar intake as much as she currently felt comfortable with to begin with. Switch over to eating more pure grains such as oats, brown rice, rye, etc and also fresh organic vegetables. Finally ditch the soda to replace it with primarily water, and bancha tea if she fancied something else. I further recommended that she add daikon (white radish) into her eating habits; this vegetable helps with breaking down fatty deposits in the body.

My advice is always intuitive, which I usually confirm by my pendulum dowsing. With Eleanor, her results became an urgent plea from me for her to change her lifestyle as quickly as she comfortably could. I sensed that if she continued along her current path, she would get really quite sick and extremely soon.

Eleanor gradually took my suggestions on board and slowly started to get her life back. Over the course of six months she weened herself off all the convenience food and soda drinks completely. She emailed that she now feels far more balanced within her moods, healthier and possesses a newfound energy and enthusiasm for life.

AGONY IN ENGLAND AND NEW YORK

There are those times when sitting down suddenly becomes imperative...

****

Visiting reputed or indeed proven famous haunted locations has never held much appeal to me. For sure I can completely understand why vast portions of the interested populous would wish to experience the thrill of a paranormal encounter, and I equally understand why such places usually have to turn people away such is the level of their waiting customers.

Encounters with the paranormal or otherworldly entities is pretty much my stock in trade and generally these days I just get actively involved if when I'm called in by anxious clients who wish to avail themselves of my services. Occasionally it is more the serendipity of a location and me; like the example given in the next chapter The Sexy Succubus!

There do exist though two occasions where I found myself intentionally visiting more touristy haunted locations, each existing on different continents and both times the same personal phenomena ensued in these separate places.

An essential ability I have learned over the decades is to switch off at least some of my direct interaction with spirit entities. I can do this more or less at will. Oh, for sure I am always acutely aware of them when in their vicinity; the necessary skill I have developed though is to leave it at just as awareness, unless I practically need to know more. If I remained an open conduit I would find it irresistible to actively interact and more than likely end up cleansing the location of the spirits or entities, which in the first of the cases I document here probably wouldn't go down terribly well the owners of the location in question.

The first occasion I knowingly ventured into a haunted property with the strongest of reputations happened to be spooky old Chingle Hall. Located near Preston, Lancashire this building has a long history of ghostly goings on. Without wishing to sound like an advert for the place, if you like ghostly old buildings this one must be worth putting on your itinerary of locations to pay a visit. Curiosity of some friends the actual reason for my own visit, with me invited along I believe to act as this walking barometer of psychic activity on their behalf!

The second paranormal hotspot I ventured into again held absolutely no interest to me at whatsoever as this potential ghostly venue. The Empire State Building in New York fascinated me at night due to the magnificent panoramic views from the 86th floor open air deck. The unfortunate souls who lost their lives jumping from the building placed far from my mind as I took some photos looking out over the metropolis.

The phenomenon afflicting me equally strongly during exploration of each of these radically different locations, paradoxically although they were not just in different continents, but hailing from seven or so centuries apart in their conception and construction, both of these places induced within me a thankfully temporary and yet quite overwhelming agony centred just in my feet!

THE SEXY SUCCUBUS!

Oliver was distraught, inconsolably distraught.

Sobbingly he collapsed right there at our feet onto the dry grass as we crowded round attempting to coax from him just what had caused his total breakdown in quite such a public and dramatic manner. Thirty seconds earlier he had staggered into view, emerging into daylight, as we all witnessed his plainly obvious terror...

****

Kiki and I travelled with a group of friends, spending part of the warm summer wandering around the ancient landscapes of Somerset, Wiltshire and Oxfordshire in England.

Oliver we hadn't known prior to the trip, he was the boyfriend of a friend. With a certain innocence he threw himself into every new area we visited with gusto and a hunger to wring every last nuance from the experience of these magical places.

The idea of this trip was to camp as close to the ancient sites as possible, walking off to explore during the day and in the evening sharing tales of our adventures or even misadventures over food at the campsite.

The first day's expedition went without any incidents. Glastonbury I had visited so times before, although new to some of our group, including Kiki. I avoided the climb up Glastonbury Tor this time, instead preferring to while away the time exploring the cornucopia of wonderful alternative shops, buying a few hippy skirts and crystals for Kiki.

The rest of the group, along with Kiki, leisurely took in the sites around Glastonbury and eventually it was time to head back to the campsite. An enjoyable, if largely unremarkable day, we duly swapped stories of our experiences and retired fairly early to our sleeping bags ready for what the next day would bring.

As morning arrived the first task became to drive over to the next campsite, erect our tents and then after these essential practicalities had been dealt with, we all headed out to explore the area surrounding Avebury in Wiltshire.

Silbury Hill stood as mysteriously enticingly as ever (sadly it is no longer possible to physically gain access to the site due to subsidence) we got as close as we were practically able, and I am sure we all felt touched on some level by the ancient past for a little while. Finally managing to tear ourselves way, slowly we made our way to the next site on our agenda. Little did we know what awaited one particular member of our group of intrepid explorers into the mysteries of our ancestor's netherworld…

Like most of the sites we were visiting I had been to West Kennet Long Barrow before. This Neolithic burial chamber once housed over forty bodies; and stands impressive in the landscape at over one hundred metres long. Inside the barrow there are four smaller chambers, two to the left and two to the right, with a larger chamber furthest down from the entrance deep inside.

OLIVER FALLS VICTIM TO THE DEMON

Oliver, in his enthusiasm to explore all these new-to-him places, had sprinted on a few hundred metres ahead of the rest of us and we saw him disappear out of site into the barrow, as in the humidity of midday sun we enjoyed a more leisurely amble up the causeway in his footsteps. And such it was as we collectively arrived a few moments later he staggered out to greet us, wearing a look of terror on his face, to subsequently collapse at our feet.

As Oliver started being able to string together some words, he told us of his experience in West Kennet Long Barrow. It was deserted as he entered the main corridor and he happily made his way further inside, grateful to escape the summer heat. Passing adjacent chambers on either side all was good with him, until he reached the second left hand chamber and then all hell broke loose. He said he felt the darkest of souls attack him; it was as if this entity had probed the deepest recesses of his mind bringing to the surface his greatest fears and making them overwhelm him in one massive psychic attack. Frozen to the spot for what seemed to him like an eternity, he was eventually able to break away and stagger back out into daylight, which is where we found him. He further claimed through tears that with absolute certainty while the entity was lodged in the barrow, he knew he would have no peace and it would haunt his dreams.

Everyone looked in my direction, my reputation having preceded me I guess. What I didn't say at this point is that, even with my experience in these matters, taking on an apparently ancient demonic entity dwelling in an equally ancient and world-famous Neolithic burial site was, shall we say, quite a tall order!

The chamber Oliver had his experience in once housed bodies. Clearly this demonic being had a powerful storehouse of psychic energy to draw upon. "Will you deal with it?" someone asked me. A nod of the head my only response as I swallowed hard in a gulp. "Once more unto the breach dear demon!" I silently thought to myself, wondering exactly what awaited me and even more importantly if it might be taken on and defeated...

THIS TIME IT'S PERSONAL!

Yet I knew I had to do this, for Oliver and anyone else who might have already fallen victim, plus any possible future souls who ventured into the barrow unprepared. I needed to free them all of this dark energy. I have a strong distaste for entities who feel it is perfectly okay to randomly attack unprotected people, keeping this at the forefront of my mind gave me the resolve to see my mission through.

In previous visits I sensed some negativity, but never felt the need to explore its recesses further, content to leave it be. Now was different, now it had attacked one of my friends, now it had become personal!

There was no need to dowse this time; I was in no doubt about what I would be dealing with. I asked Kiki to please wait outside, she didn't want to, but I needed to protect her from what I was about to do.

Nobody met my eyes as I walked towards the entrance to the barrow and then onwards to whatever awaited me. Too late for me to now change my mind. I knew the entity would already be fully aware of my presence and like everyone else; it was waiting to see what I would do next...

Making my way to the second left hand chamber immediately the dark force tried to attack me, seeking to catch me off guard before I was ready, oppressively it pressed down upon me. My world becoming dark, I knew I must remain calm and unhurried.

I instinctively felt the need to be in complete direct contact with the stones this barrow was constructed out of. I carefully sat myself down in the lotus position directly in the centre of the icily freezing cold stone plinth in the chamber Oliver had his experience in for complete physical contact to the essence of the barrow. Just the way I knew it needed to be. As the ancient stones met with my derrière and my bare legs (I wore shorts) the shock caused me to involuntarily shiver for quite a few moments to the point of my body actually shaking. It felt exactly like sitting down on an iceberg shipped in directly from the Artic!

The all-enveloping negativity continued to rage all around me and so putting my frozen numb posterior out of my mind, in my time-honoured way I closed my eyes and controlled my breathing to go into a meditation.

A cloying, pitch black maelstrom surrounded and probed me as in another reality I began to contact, as it turned out to be, the female demon…apparently an actual genuine succubus it would seem, and oh my gosh she was too seriously sexy! Then that's what they are all about. In all of my experience this was my first-time of coming face to face with a real succubus, although fully aware of what they can do, sexy or not, I sensed I might just be able to deal with her.

Let battle commence!

The succubus was distinctly displeased at my presence and trying her best to seduce me with her power. I could sense she was beginning to become wary of me being unafraid and inability to be manipulated. And she threw everything she could at me, she tried everything in her armoury to put me under her spell or get me to leave. Attack after attack, and yet with every attempt I learned more and more about her and the portal she used to visit our world.

In the right circumstances an ancient site such as that acts rather like this powerful generator, channelling the way for creatures which have no right to be here in our world to interact and feed off the very fear they create. Paradoxically growing in strength, gaining an ever more terrifying ability to interact with those it senses are easy prey. My task was to send this demon back from whence she came and to seal off the portal for her or any of her friends to be able to pay return visit...well at least not through West Kennet Long Barrow!

On one level of consciousness I was still able to sense normal life going on outside of the battle, other visitors exploring the site and thankfully giving the chamber I was housed in a nice wide berth. Meanwhile in another dimension it became the moment for me to strike back against this anomaly. I could psychically now see Sexy Succubus's gateway to her netherworld, pushing the demon back step by step it got closer to this portal. She retreated slightly, gathering strength (most likely from victims such as Oliver), I knew this was probably my only chance and oh boy I went for it…virtually bundling her through the portal in one powerful energy kick and immediately sealing it, closing off any possible counter-attack.

Silence descended.

The sounds of drumming and chanting broke through the silence as I came out my meditation. All perception of time leaves me during session such as this. Opening my eyes I found myself looking straight into those of my old friend John Ram. Of all my friends he is the only one I trusted to sufficiently psychically protected to follow me into the long barrow. John told me it had not been more than twenty minutes since I first entered the long barrow. Using his pendulum, he quickly dowsed, with his results confirming the demonic entity gone.

Climbing from out of my chamber I chose to explore the source of music, finding three folk musicians in the main chamber taking advantage of the superb acoustics for an impromptu jamming session. And strangely their music started immediately after I accomplished the banishment, looking them in the eyes while they played and chanted, I knew they knew what I had done. One of them smiled at me and I smiled back, no words required.

Suddenly feeling exhausted, I turned and took my leave of the long barrow.

What of Oliver? As I emerged back into daylight, he stood waiting for me. He grinned as he enveloped me in a long tight hug. Believe me I really knew I had been hugged when he eventually let me go! Oliver was back with us, a little more cautious now perhaps, yet free of any dark presence or influence.

He would stay close by me during the rest of our travels as he said he felt safer, although I repeatedly reassured him there really was no need. I heard through the grapevine he returned home with no further problems and life continued as usual for him.

LEGACY

I do think sometimes of West Kennet Long Barrow, especially if I hear of someone I know paying a visit. The enormity of the task I took on that day, how it might have all ended so differently. I guess the fact I didn't have time to consider other options and, like I so oftentimes seem to end up being compelled to, I just dived straight in and dealt with the negative entity is why it all worked out as it did. A little of my personal energy remains in that barrow and any future visitors who are sensitive to psychic phenomena will feel this. Forever changing the energy of this world-famous Megalithic monument is about as big as it gets – at least the innocent and unprotected are now safe to enjoy the site.

SELF-PERPETUATED DESPAIR

"I have heard you help people with strange problems Sir" he murmured, looking around making sure to not be overheard. "It has been known" as I smiled disarmingly and asked "What exactly is your problem?" His reply got my full attention "I think I've been cursed!"

****

As I might have mentioned, I resolutely believe some people cross our paths for a reason, point of fact I have had this said to me on many occasions and meeting Ash was a serendipitous happening. Deeply unhappy, over a cup of herbal tea his troubles came tumbling forth from out of him. Glad he was to be afforded the opportunity to unburden himself of things he had lived with inside for nearly two years.

Ash had been unemployed for over eighteen months, although he was keen to find work and armed with two qualifications to his name, one in plumbing and the other social work, every interview he attended ended the same way. No job.

There had been a family feud a couple of years before, Ash had three sisters, he was the only male child and the second youngest sibling. His older sisters had taken exception to something he had done and as these things are sometimes prone to do, the situation had escalated to the point where his eldest sister said he was no longer her brother and cut him out of her life completely.

Shortly after this he lost his job and felt compelled to move to another town in an attempt to put things behind him and start over again. Ash with absolute conviction believed his eldest sister had cursed him and his bad luck ever since acted as a self-fulfilling confirmation to him that this must indeed be the case. He told me he felt like a magnet for bad things and negative happenings in his life. He had lost his career and more tellingly his self-respect. He asked if I might help him and we parted with me saying I would see what I could do.

Spiritual healing always gets to the heart of the matter and in this case, it was about guilt created self-sabotage. As is my method, I removed the energy associated with these feelings Ash carried around with him.

Taking away negative energy doesn't guarantee to also take away the issue, what it does though is free the individual to leave it behind if they are ready. Of course, the timing must be right, if the feelings run really deeply within a person, removing any negativity will only be temporary, they always being freely able to build up all those bad feelings all over again. Such is free-will.

Ash knew through his actions he had offended senior members of his family, and whilst on a conscious level he stood alone in his new town sincerely looking for work yet feeling depressed and awful about his life. On a subconscious level he felt guilty and unworthy of any success. It didn't matter where geographically he went; those feelings would travel right there with him.

The healing session completed I awaited news of Ash and, although having not arranged another meeting at that point, I knew our paths would cross again soon. He was for sure open to change and I pondered how that might have manifested for him

A month passed by until this by chance (but inevitable) meeting took place. All smiles and hand outstretched ready to shake mine, I bumped into Ash as I walked off stage from a speaking engagement. Asking how life was for him, I was delighted to hear he had been taken on by a kitchen installation company as a plumber and more than that, his mother had arranged a family clear-the-air meeting in the next few days! His sisters all said they would attend and they were keen for reconciliation.

Our paths rarely cross now; my work with Ash is done. I did hear he decided to go back part-time to University and gain a degree in civil engineering. I wish him every success. I have the feeling he will pass with first class honours.

THE SWAMP CREATURE FROM HELL!

"Any chance you might have a look at our café?" the email candidly asked, without caring to give too much information away as to exactly the reason why they felt I ought to. A succinct one-word question from me asked in my return email, quite simply "Why?" The answer proved irresistible "Well, there's something creepy haunting us and we think it never was actually human!"

****

The café concerned had already been in operation for quite a few years before it came to my attention. Built on an ancient main road into the city, buildings existed on this same plot going back hundreds of years. The café was housed in a property itself I estimated must be at least a hundred years old, before that there would have certainly been another structure preceding it and so on back through the centuries.

Adjacent to the café stood an even older disused factory mill building, dark and damp with filthy windows placed tantalizingly slightly above even my head height, offering no clues as to what the interior might be like. Why this prime piece of real estate hadn't been snapped-up by a property speculator was a mystery. Conversion into flats, as befell so many other mills, seemed only a planning application away.

The café, alongside its neighbour the old factory, sat positioned exactly at the top end of a long-reclaimed former wetland area known as Marsh Lane. Apparently the original streams still ran underground channelled down far beneath the road and all the way down to the river.

I arrived during a weekday to find the café staff busily occupied with serving customers. Eventually in the mid-afternoon lull I managed to have the conversation I had gone there for. All the members of staff had their own experiences to tell of their uninvited guest. Chairs moving on their own in the café when all was quiet and dishes crashing down in the kitchen; plus, strange smells permeating the air to the rear area of the premises where the patio gardens and al-fresco dining area sat.

Everyone shared their feelings of foreboding walking down the passage, past the washrooms, out to the aforementioned dining area at the rear of the building. They imagined they must have a poltergeist. I keep an open mind on any investigations; walking the passage myself for sure it felt oppressively heavy and foreboding, yet I did sense something else there as well.

I stayed around all afternoon observing until the café closed at 6pm. I already asked if it would be possible to stay on after for a while there by myself. Confirming this, Brad (the contact who so enigmatically emailed me) told me he would pull down the shutters to lock me in for a few hours, returning later at 9pm to release me.

DISCOVERING MORE

After the last customer left and the dishes were being washed, I sat down with Brad to establish if there might be anything else he could share with me before my lock-down began...

Sat in the empty café, and where no customers might accidentally overhear, he mentioned over the last couple of months they thought they must have an issue with mice (clearly not good news for a café!). Staff members thought they caught sight of scurrying mice out of the corner of their eye, yet no face-to-face encounter had yet occurred. Furthermore, strangely no evidence of any droppings or food disturbance; having put out humane traps overnight, so far the mice had eluded all attempts at capture.

It never ceases to amaze me how an investigation can seem to be on the face of it one thing and, now armed as I was with the information about mice, turns around completely to be altogether more unusual and far rarer. I had encountered shadow-mice as part of another case a few years prior to this one and evidence now appeared to point towards one particular kind of haunting or manifestation.

I kept all this to myself at this point. I never speculate on anything to my client before an investigation.

THE INVESTIGATION

As metal shutters were locked, silence descended. I stood stock-still in the centre of the café…listening with my intuition.

I wasn't about to call-out this particular entity. Not just yet. Firstly there was someone entirely different I needed to attend to. A matter of duty you might call it. Then, later I would move on to the bigger issue plaguing the café. First I had to deal with the lost spirit occupying the corridor to the outside dining area!

Opening the door into the passage to enter in total darkness, I made my silent way along to where I knew the epicentre of the paranormal activity to be located. I never intentionally work in darkness, in my experience it makes precious little difference if it is broad daylight or the pitch black of night, if there is some spirit or entity present it is going to be there whatever. On this occasion, as I had my eyes closed anyway, there practically didn't seem much point in turning on the light.

The location I sought was exactly halfway down the corridor. To the left stood a locked door and asking earlier I knew all that lay behind it was a cupboard housing extra supplies for the washroom and spare cleaning materials for the kitchen. For some reason the spirit was attached to this door and what lay beyond it. I definitely sensed psychically a cupboard wasn't always really where this door once led. The thought I had is that it might well have long ago been a door to steps leading down to a long-forgotten cellar (I was never able to confirm this, although Brad later agreed it made sense).

I reached out and immediately the spirit of the man I wanted to help made himself known. Scared and lost, this young man didn't even take the opportunity to share with me any of his story. I simply opened a way for him to the light; far from this place in the 1960's accidentally become attached to. He virtually leapt at the opportunity, and as so often happens, I felt a wave of peace and gratitude flood over me.

Okay, having freed the trapped spirit and seemingly all in less than ten minutes now for the bigger picture, now for the real beast...commonly known as a Boggart!

A Boggart is a usually malevolent non-human spirit to be found in marsh like areas (bogs, hence the name) or in buildings built on top of these locations. Hardly the most pleasant of creatures to share any space with, they are smelly and as their natural habitat is wetland, they bring this darkly depressing and damply cloying energy with them.

My reason for coming to the conclusion I was dealing with a Boggart, rather than another manifestation, (such as the suggested Poltergeist) had a lot to do with mice...

On my previous investigation in another area, also in a building built on former marshland, shadow-mice had been encountered. In this case even to the point of the property owner thinking he had humanely caught them, taking the trouble to carry them far away to another place, only to discover them right back there again the following day.

In my experience then everything pointed to a Boggart being the likely cause of the activity and in all honesty this actually led to quite an issue for me.

In my previous case I had found the Boggart impossible to deal with through applying any of my established usual methods. In fact my suggestion to the residents in the end had been to move to a new house someplace else!

They would follow my advice such was the level of their desperation, and I offered them protection ensuring the Boggart didn't follow them, as this can be all too real a possibility. A Boggart can become attached to a certain human and are incredibly difficult to shake-off, unless they subsequently lose interest themselves.

I walked back into the main area of the café and turned all the lights on right throughout the place from behind the counter. It was time to make contact. First though I needed to find the thing!

A Boggart isn't always too willing to sit down over a latte for a chat. They are something of a paranormal law unto themselves. Mostly existing in a different level of reality than ours, yet finding it an irresistible temptation to interact, usually unseen, with humans they encounter. They arrogantly also seem to be all too aware there is precious little even the more experienced investigator, such as myself, can do in reality to stop them.

Quite why they are immune to those like me is perhaps not a great mystery. A Boggart is a type of water spirit whose natural environment is swamps, lakes, and even sometimes slow flowing rivers. Alien territory to us in every way. The last time I encountered one it felt rather like attempting to reason with a spectacularly stroppy teenager, who also happened to be fully aware he didn't have to listen to me anyway!

On occasions I dowse to detect particularly secretive paranormal phenomena, this café investigation became just such a time. Using my pendulum, this time I had my favourite reclaimed wood one with me, as I sought the epicentre of all the activity or more accurately from whence the Boggart came!

Moving from the customer area, through the kitchen, no conclusive dowsing results, this creature was either unbelievably well shielded or this wasn't the area I needed to be looking. I favoured the latter conclusion…

On to the formerly haunted corridor, I followed my pendulum which gravitated me down to the back door leading onto the garden and the outdoor seating area. Silently offering blessings to Brad for leaving the door unlocked, outside I ventured. More reaction now from my pendulum, I must be getting close. And for sure a pungent odour now assaulted my senses, like rotting vegetation mixed with stagnant water. Exploring the well-lit outside area and still following my pendulum I found myself opening a gate which clearly led to a part of the complex kept hidden from the gaze of diners.

Wow, I had metaphorically struck gold!

On the one side this little yard housed the catering sized trash cans for the café, on the other though the inner wall of the adjacent unused mill building lay revealed and this time much lower placed windows enabled me to catch a glimpse inside. Dereliction, decay, damp, and water still dripping down the walls from the recent rain, all in all there stood the perfect home from home for a Boggart! I put my pendulum away, as now I had found him, so what to do next?

Doing what I do requires absolute belief in my abilities to suitably deal with whatever might cross my path. Apprehension and fear are my enemies, self-defeating enemies, leading to vulnerability some of the less moral entities I occasionally encounter would love to feed off. I have used strong psychic self-protection ever since my teenage years, built up over the decades to the point where, although in theory I am still liable to be attacked, I generally find paranormal nasties are more wary of me than me of them!

The Boggart wasn't in the slightest bit wary or in any way respecting of me or any other humans. From his perspective humans were pests to taunt and tease. Thankfully I would discover he wasn't truly malevolent like his cousin I met some years earlier, more in a sense world-weary, and practically sick of humans.

MEET SIR BOGGART!

Sir Boggart (as he apparently liked to be known) had existed far back into distant antiquity, long before any of these old buildings had stood and when the whole area was marshland. Humans had come along and drained his home, putting their stain on his landscape with their streets and structures. He wasn't best pleased, although over the centuries hate had tempered into his final resignation at the way things were.

Eventually he retreated into the old mill building to make it his lair. Equally ensuring that he remained undisturbed and his home free of what he considered to be human infestation; he managed most effectively to spook any curious property speculators venturing into his domain.

Please be aware the previous paragraph is based on the intuitive details able to be gathered during my time spent in the psychic company of Sir Boggart. One does not simply have a conversation with a Boggart but when connecting to an entity such as this, a certain amount of latent information does pass back and forth. It wasn't in any way pleasant communicating with him (intrusive hate mingled with arrogant contempt more or less sums it up) being thought of as best just another human pest doesn't really give the best position to be negotiating or bargaining from!

Mice were one of the ways he liked to tease humans; aware of the function of the café it amused him to manifest shadow-mice to scare the staff. He stalked the café, they disturbed his peace with their outside garden and dining area, alarmingly I sensed he'd got far more extreme manifestations in store soon for Brad and his customers...

I sent forth this suggestion to him - how about if the outside area were to be left unused and free of human pests? How about this space became off-limits to the café patrons and if he allowed the staff to use the little yard adjoining his den once a day to dispose of rubbish, there would end any further intrusion.

Wondering on one level of my consciousness how Brad might react to seeing his seating area for customers now being halved due to his beautiful garden becoming off limits! I had no idea at all if Sir Boggart agreed to my proposed compromise as he didn't deign to respond and withdrew from contact.

IT IS DONE...

My work there was done. Returning to the main café I made myself a basil tea and awaited freedom in the form of Brad unlocking the shutters.

In due course the opportunity came to share my experiences with Brad; and furthermore, putting my proposal to him to establish if it might work for him in some way. Commendable calmness would be my overriding memory of his response. Satisfied with the compromise, he chose to take on board my suggestions and he further informed me from opening the following morning the rear outside dining area would be "closed for refurbishment" as far as all his customers were concerned.

I had one more final recommendation, and this was the same one I had made once before in a Boggart case, please move to relocate!

I left them all to it and asked to be kept informed of events unfolding. A few weeks later an email arrived. All had been quiet, no more bangs and crashes and the corridor felt much more pleasant to use. The mice had also gone; the other news Brad wanted to share is he had found larger premises in a similar part of the city, but away from Marsh Lane.

DROPPING BY FOR AN UPDATE

Around a year on Kiki and I paid a visit to the new café. Brad told us his business was booming. They had established an all-new garden with al-fresco dining area and rather wonderfully no Boggart to disturb anyone.

With Brad fully occupied talking with Kiki (She has that effect on people, her eyes are mesmeric and the woman is beyond merely gorgeous) I took myself off for a solo tour of the place Upon my return in a fifteen minutes I saw Brad comprehensively under the spell of my Kiki; I broke the enchantment by confirming the cafe an ancient swamp-dwelling creature free zone.

As the new space felt so right to staff and customers I kept it to myself that in reality they shared this new building with many spirits. As all concerned co-existed happily enough there didn't seem any particular reason to mention it.

SOUL-STEALING DEMON

A Wendigo is a cannibalistic evil spirit and shape-shifting master of disguise reputedly native to Canada and northern parts of the USA. Why then were reports reaching me of one being free to wreak havoc in Preston, England? I needed to know more…

****

Two independent sources had been quoted and found their way to me, as the unusual and weird often does. They were quite sure that a Wendigo had somehow managed to manifest in the northern England City of Preston, as far as I could ascertain they were quite sincere in their claims and genuinely believed this to be the case.

Whenever approaching any kind of investigation I keep my mind open to any possibility, experience has taught me things are rarely as they might first seem to be and having been witness to some pretty far-out stuff over the years, this level-headed approach I am sure has saved my sanity on more than one occasion. Nevertheless, the thought of a Wendigo and the implications surrounding their really well-founded reputation for devouring our immortal souls did cause me to metaphorically raise an eyebrow if not in scepticism, then perhaps at least with a willingness to hope and believe this couldn't possibly genuinely be the case!

There are woods to the south of the river which bisects the city; it was in these woods and around the bridge crossing over the river where the apparent sightings had occurred. Late night revellers talked of their terrifying encounters in the early hours of the morning on their journey home.

These woods are located beyond the river and run up a hill to the graveyard of a local church. I was already aware of the nature spirits dwelling in the protection of the trees in the woods, feeling their presence at another time on previous explorations in the area as part of a different investigation. Apart from occasionally having a little mischievous fun at the expense of human visitors straying onto their patch, such as twanging branches into people or tripping them up to fall into the mud, they didn't cause any real harm and I happily left them in peace.

A potential Wendigo though was in a different ballpark all together!

TWO WISE MEN

I sought out Guy, the local prophet and seer. We had crossed paths a few times before. A conversation shared with Guy is certainly always entertaining and suitably abstractly off-the–wall. He is sensitive to energy changes, often telling usually sceptically disbelieving people he encounters exactly what the energy in his city is like on any given day. Talking with him confirmed he felt sure there was indeed something like a Wendigo and he was determined to confront it as soon as possible. "Would you mind not doing yet, Guy?" I asked him. I needed to go and see for myself, the last thing I needed was a well-meaning man like Guy stirring things up and polluting my findings. He knew what they could do and declared he was willing to sacrifice himself for the greater good of everyone else; laudable and courageous though this was it wasn't part of *my* plans for any souls to get lost to whatever evil manifestation had decided to pay Preston a visit. After much persuasion, Guy agreed to back off at least until after I had done a little investigating of my own. He offered to go investigate with me…I declined. I work alone.

It often isn't, but when it is actually possible I like to gather as much information as available to me prior to engaging directly in any investigation. Sometimes there is no choice and on those occasions I just have to go and dive right in to see what transpires. In this case there existed another source apart from Guy; one other person I knew I could trust would tell me the facts as he saw them.

John Ram we met in The Sexy Succubus chapter. He is one of my oldest friends, who kindly mentored me as a young naive psychic for a few years from when we first met. I respect and love him. A much revered wise-man who is incredibly attuned to his environment and the earth. A conversation with John is always gripping. I asked him if he thought there might be some dark forces at work in or around the city. Calmly he pondered, his far-seeing eyes seemingly reaching out into the very the landscape. "Yes, there is something" he softly declared. Knowing him well, I knew he would say as much as he knew and speculate no further. Asking if he felt it might be a Wendigo, I was met with his calmly silent gaze and a shrug of shoulders, followed by a change of subject.

Short of going out on the street to interview passers-by I possessed as much information as I was ever likely to be able to arm myself with. I needed to get more hands-on!

I GO WENDIGO HUNTING!

Night-time investigations to me are frankly a bit of a cliché, in my experience it doesn't matter greatly in personal contact cases if it is broad daylight or night. On this occasion, however, I ventured to the river a little after 1am. The main reason being there were likely to be less people around and so if I did stir up any kind of paranormal nasty, I would be free to deal with it without any likelihood of getting interrupted. The secondary reason is the reported cases of witnessing the creature had all occurred late at night or early in the morning...

Walking along the banks of the river and over the bridge all seemed normal, oh for sure a few spirits roamed, yet nothing of the magnitude I was seeking.

Sensing the need to probe deeper and knowing if this genuinely was a Wendigo it would need some kind of den with access to much psychic energy. The church and graveyard seemed the obvious choice. Atmospheric and eerie, I found my careful way through the mist strewn graveyard to an elevated grassy mound known as Castle Hill, overlooking the river, woods and graves.

Noises stirred all around me as silently I climbed the hill, becoming aware of the curious nature spirits down in the woods there below me wanting to know what I was doing, I ignored them and concentrated on reaching out psychically

I guess I must have looked more than a little strange to anyone who might have happened upon me at 2am. Unusually for me on this occasion, and because it had felt right to me on that night, I was dressed in all black. I stood there on the peak of this small hill overlooking the misty graveyard, my arms raised above my head, eyes closed and standing stock still, psychically probing into the ethers.

If any insomniac dog-walkers did witness me I wasn't aware of it. If they did perhaps they took me to be some ghostly shadow figure haunting the graveyard.

I searched on every level and yet of the Wendigo I could find no trace, plenty of spirits, but no soul devouring ogre out of most persons worst nightmares came to say hello to me! After 3am passed on by, I called it off and headed away...

I had come back with a complete zero in my search for a Wendigo, yet I knew the witnesses must clearly have seen something, to me it now became more a question of exactly what? To solve this I concluded was going to require a far more sledgehammer approach, as my more subtle invite to come along and have a chat with me hadn't worked.

DAYTIME AND A FACE-TO-FACE ENCOUNTER

Two days later saw me sitting meditating down by the riverbank in the pleasant spring afternoon sun. As unremarkable a scene as you could imagine, apart from the beauty of sunlight reflecting off the water and birds singing in the trees.

Opening myself up I called out, challenging his creature, if it was out there, to come and take me on...ready to do battle, if a little unsure exactly what to expect if it did indeed turn out to be a Wendigo...as always I needed to do this.

Suddenly it rushed towards me, seems my challenge had done the trick. Now to see what I had taken on. Was it some horribly dark force of pure evil or perhaps even a creature ready to devour my very soul?

A Trickster! Not some Wendigo, but a Trickster creating havoc and frightening those who had enjoyed a few too many drinks out of their skin while they made their unsteady late-night way home.

Like a Wendigo, Tricksters can also shape-shift; the big difference is their pleasure comes from scaring people witless, rather than more or less eating them.

Although one can never trust a Trickster, it is possible to reason with them and I do believe its intentions were to show the drunken people the error of their ways. Or perhaps I am overstating the case, whatever, after our encounter I have heard no further reports of a Wendigo on the loose. Although I can't say for sure it doesn't still happen that maybe some inebriated revellers returning home after a night-out might still encounter something, the experience of which may well make them sober up remarkably quickly...

MY KINGDOM FOR A...

Stephanie told me her best friend Robbie lay seriously ill, tragically he had not been given any kind of hope by all the medical experts and she asked "can you help him?" I suggested "although I can obviously make no promises I will certainly do a distant healing and see what I see, but please ask him first if Robbie is okay with me doing this". Stephanie explained further "he's been off his food, sleeping a lot and by the way, you do know that Robbie is my horse?"

****

I had known Stephanie for over a decade having first met her through mutual friend Terrance who she dated for a short while. We possessed more than Terrance in common; as occasionally happens we clicked straight away as good friends and although we didn't see each other perhaps more than once a year, we kept in touch often via email. Stephanie and I realised we did share many similar threads in our lives, and although she and Terrance split-up shortly after my meeting her, our own relationship has only ever been about our psychic connection and the easy friendship that exists between the two of us.

And so it was if she ever felt herself in the need of my particular kind of help she felt free to contact me to ask. Such a time occurred when she shared with me all about Robbie, her best friend.

His body was wearing out it would seem. He slept a lot and had precious little appetite. She had already called in all the equine experts and unfortunately, they equally proclaimed his condition untreatable, telling her it was simply down to his age and it would only be a matter of a short time before he passed.

This is just about where I came in...

Stephanie emailed, and subsequently we spoke. She told me everything about his condition and quite wrongly I assumed Robbie must be an older friend or perhaps a relative, such was the level of affection she clearly possessed for him and the way she described her broken emotional state at the thought of losing him. I must confess to getting a little shocked upon finally being informed I was to treat a horse!

Reassuring Stephanie, and making no promises as to any level of success I might achieve, I resolved to do a series of distant psychic healings for Robbie.

At this point in my development I had never actually treated any kind of animal before, this was to be an entirely new experience and I sincerely had no idea what possible results (if indeed any) I might be able to achieve.

I told Stephanie we would talk around a week from our last conversation, leave me to do my stuff and then she would be able to bring me up to date about the situation with Robbie.

Consulting my dowsing pendulum seemed like a good option at this point. I asked the following two questions:

1. Can I heal Robbie? (No)

2. Can I help Robbie to feel more comfortable (Yes)

This is all I needed to know!

Putting myself into my usual meditative state, for the very first time I attempted making a psychic connection with a horse for a healing session. And found I was quite able to. Truth be told it wasn't significantly different to healing for a human...for the next six days my daily routine became at the same time to psychically connect to Robbie and gently work on easing his suffering.

After the week passed by the promised phone call came from Stephanie. I waited with bated breath for news of my equine friend of a friend. She told me he seemed considerably more himself, he had started eating a little and to her delight she had been able to take him for a short walk in the paddock where he was stabled. She was under no illusions he was still in the twilight of his life, all she truly wished for was Robbie is that he got to live out his final days without pain.

Stephanie got her wish.

Robbie perked up considerably, now able to eat properly, some of his former strength returned. Stephanie was able to take him for a gentle walk two or three times a week. They absolutely were indeed the best of friends; she emailed me photos of them together and he would stroll beside her along bridleways and nuzzle her with his head.

Robbie and Stephanie enjoyed all that summer to share precious time together. He finally passed in late October of the same year; quietly he went in his sleep. Stephanie told me she will always treasure that summer...

KIKI IS UNIMPRESSED

"I think our new home might be haunted babe" Kiki had tentatively suggested to me on the day after we moved in, searching my face hoping for me to confirm to her it was all down to an overactive imagination. "Oh, for sure it is Kiki, I know all about Albert" followed my happy reply. This did nothing at all to reassure Kiki, eliciting her rather loud response "For crying out loud babe! You of ALL people let us move into a haunted house!!!"

****

For nearly a whole year we had talked of moving home, yet equally so we knew it had to feel right and up to that point it surely hadn't. Always trusting to the right events happening at the right time, patiently we waited. Eventually everything fell into place with unmistakable synchronicity, giving us every indication we might have wished for, finally the moment for action had arrived.

We only travelled to view two potential new homes in the end and, without consciously planning it that way; they turned out to be situated next door to one another! The first one didn't have quite the right vibe, nothing particularly jarred with us, yet we knew it wasn't to be our next home. The cottage next door to it though was perfect…it even had a cute den-space for me!

The moment we ventured inside we knew here we had found it. Immediately I became aware of our (unseen by Kiki or the estate agent) resident spirit house guest, Albert. Really personally speaking I wasn't concerned, not viewing him as any kind of threat or issue, knowing he was only curious and meant no harm to us. A deal was duly done and shortly after we held the keys to our new cottage in our hand.

We allowed ourselves a short while personalizing the place with some essential re-decorating and installing fitted furniture prior to moving in. Spending time alone I was able to communicate to learn more of Albert, a little of his story and way he felt it necessary to stay around in the cottage.

The cottage lay empty for around three years, having undergone a radical update and modernisation during that time. Albert then was the previous owner and felt extremely protective of his home; I sensed he needed to stay around in order to ensure everything was okay with the improvements. As it had stood vacant for so long, he was having difficulty in letting go of his responsibility and stayed on as effectively care-taker of the property, such was his level of attachment.

Our first night in our new home lived up to everything we dreamed of, here finally we had our space precisely how we always wanted it to be. The only downside had occurred when Kiki rose in the morning to head towards the bathroom. As she passed along the upper hall out of the corner of her eye, she momentarily glimpsed a male figure stood near the second bedroom door. Dismissing it as just her over fertile imagination, her vision later that same day became more validated when she witnessed a similar apparition in the kitchen. She didn't want to share our home with the previous occupant and rather uncompromisingly asked me what I would be doing about it!

Explaining the truth as I understood it about Albert calmed her a little. Speaking directly to him she thanked him for looking after the cottage and left the situation in my hands. Kiki trusted in my ability to deal with the matter in the nicest way possible.

About a week later found me meditating in our bedroom. I gradually became aware of Albert around me and reached out to him. I reassured him that his work here was done, his home now resided in our safe hands and we would happily look after it exactly as he would have wished. If he would like to move-on he could do so now and let his obligation go.

I felt overwhelming peace emanating around the room and then he was gone. He never returned, which we both agree feels rather beautiful that he trusts us enough to know that we will all treasure our home as much as he did...

INTRODUCTION TO MEETING MY NEMESIS

The particular day in question saw me at a bit of a loose end and looking for something interesting to do. As I mentioned more than once in these pages, I passionately believe the experiences we have through life happen for a reason. Especially those episodes that find us face to face with the unexpected and frequently our own fears. Through these moments we are offered the opportunity to firstly realise perhaps we didn't know as much as we once thought, and secondly we are now presented with an incredible opportunity to grow as a person.

Part One - The action takes place in 2013, although in an reality the actual date or year is largely irrelevant, as you will see.

At that time I made a firm commitment to re-visit this location at a later date, when I felt more able to remain detached and protected from whatever deeply terrifying occurrences I feared that I would once more experience.

Part Two - This time in we are in 2018. That it took me five years to return hardly surprises me. The revelations from this second adventure left a few more unanswered questions; and yet for all that I do feel I understand more of what the location is all about now.

Come and join me for one last adventure together in this book...

MEETING MY NEMESIS PART ONE (2013)

Unfamiliar, yet quite overwhelming terror overtook my senses. One chance of escape opened up before me and without pausing for another second of consideration survival instinct took over as I immediately set off wildly sprinting as fast as I was able…

****

This pleasant autumn day saw me exploring for pleasure, my diary being more or less free of anything requiring any urgent attention, off I sallied forth to Lancaster in northern Lancashire, England. Having happily rambled in and out the city shops for an hour, I started to look around for something else to do.

There is a Castle in Lancaster, which up until not so long ago had existed to be a jail, and the history of such use stretches back over several centuries. Tours are offered of the former cells and many do find the temptation irresistible; for sure this building is reputed to be incredibly haunted and the thrill of such an experience usually means the tours are well attended.

Not for me though. Given my area of activity, to intentionally go seeking a ghostly encounter just for the sake of it certainly seemed rather pointless. At the time I likened it to someone working in a bank spending their day-off watching other people working in a bank or a rock band going to a concert by another rock band in-between their gigs. So it was I passed on the pleasure of a visit to Lancaster Castle and instead began making my way up to Williamson Park.

This park is located to the east of the city, sat up on the very top of a hill. The views from there are spectacular, overlooking firstly as it does right across the whole of Lancaster and then carrying on to the further distant Morecambe Bay and the sea. Covering nearly fifty-five acres this beautifully landscaped park-on-a-hill houses the iconic Ashton Memorial building (seen from the M6 motorway when passing by Lancaster) and plenty of woodland areas to explore. The lure of which is why half an hour later, after walking steeply uphill from the city centre, I duly arrived to pay homage to both nature and the park.

When not much more than a baby my parents would bring me to Williamson Park, we had family who lived in Lancaster and a visit to them would invariably see us at some point heading up the hill and onto the park. Although any sense of nostalgia being far from the reason for my visit on that day, I did nevertheless find it amusing to walk for a while in the footsteps my earlier smaller self once toddled all those years before.

I visited the resident café in the centre of the park for a refreshing herbal tea and then suitably sustained, I went to explore a little further off the more well-worn track and deep into the dense woodland I ventured.

Making my way between trees while avoiding sinking up to my ankles in the soft mud, not another human was to be seen or heard, only the birds and other woodland creatures going about their natural routine. Sometimes this is exactly the way I like it to be, I feel a beautiful sense of freedom to occasionally spend time absolutely alone in nature and this being such an experience it was food to my soul. The same reason I am also to be found going for walks deep in the heart of winter along the same beaches which in summer would be resplendent with several thousand holiday makers, but at that time deserted due to the torrential rain or blizzard I am rather enjoying!

They say that all detectives find their nemesis, that one case they cannot crack or the criminal who eludes them – it is certainly the same with paranormal investigators and indeed psychic healers. There will inevitably be that single location or even a energy healing where they will experience immediate conflict with; and so despite their best efforts they are unable to deal with the situation to any satisfactory outcome. Although blissfully unaware at that point, right there in Williamson Park my nemesis awaited me…

Venturing deeper into the otherworldly woods, further away from all the main pathways, suddenly a pair of beautiful large gothic metal gates stood before me. Looking for all the world like the gates at the entrance to a cemetery, standing about two and a half metres in height by three metres at wide and evidently quite old. Through them I glimpsed the dilapidated remains of what looked to have once been a substantial building.

Finding a gap in the gates wide enough to squeeze through, naturally in I went to explore. Overgrown and with a pervading odour of damp, carefully I made my way over to the left-hand side of all that remained of the building, intending to walk clockwise around what looked like a cloister. Strolling down the natural corridor of the cloister I quickly became all too aware that I was no longer alone!

A tall presence followed me, when I say followed, more accurately looming menacingly right over me stalked the weirdest of entities I had ever encountered.

And this wasn't some run of the mill ordinary ghostly presence or indeed any variety of elemental being I had experienced before. No, this thing, whatever it may have been, elicited within me an instantaneous reaction of

161

pure unadulterated terror beginning from the pit of my stomach and passing out through every cell of my body. And as it towered over me from just a few centimetres behind, I could feel its threatening presence touching me!

Quickening my pace, I turned right at the far corner on the left side to continue along the back of the building. I realised genuine real danger existed here and getting away suddenly became imperative. The need to escape became all consuming. As sheer panic overwhelmed me I knew I had but one opportunity to escape and only the one...

Throwing every last gram of psychic self-protection outwardly in a massive projection of personal power or chi, I did all I could do under the circumstances, as I shouted "Geronimo" at the top of my lungs and ran as fast as I could!

Sprinting flat out I covered the entire length of the right-hand wing of the building in the matter of what must have been a few seconds to reach the welcoming site of the gates. Running as I was at full pelt, I still managed to spot the gap I entered through and so without slowing down I literally dived headfirst through this same gap in the gates, and out of that terrifying place.

Slowly, as I collected myself up from all the brambles and mud I had unceremoniously landed face first in, I offered silent thanks to the goddess that in the morning I had chosen to wear jeans and trainers on the day rather than shorts and sandals. I then reflected on how I knew on some level of my consciousness that getting out of there and past those gates would render me safe. Satisfied my psychic self-protection still existed intact and equally satisfied the spirit creature from the depths of hell had stayed within the confines of the building, I rapidly bid my bramble prickled muddy goodbye to Williamson Park. I went back down the hill to Lancaster, found my car and headed home with many questions.

Growing-up being fully aware there exists far more than only the three-dimensional world we all take for granted prepared the way for me as an adult with my life of helping others; both humans or animals through psychic healing and also either assisting errant spirits to pass through over to the other side or sending otherworldly entities with no right to co-exist with us back to where they belong. Having quite literally tackled ghosts and nasties head-on over many years, experiencing a personally terrifying encounter upon a wooded hillside had definitely proved to be a new one to me! I needed to know more and crucially what exactly it might have been I actually encountered.

THE MYSTERY DEEPENS

I will share next exactly what I have since been able to find out about Williamson Park, and the dark history overshadowing that area; a then make my supposition about what the entity I encountered might be and the nature of the experience I went through on that day.

Lancaster Castle, as I mentioned, existed for several centuries in one form or another as a prison. During the era of capital punishment hangings would take place there, however, before the year 1800 the ultimate sentence would be carried out at this place known as Gallows Hill. Much debate exists about the precise location of these gallows. What is undisputed though is for the population of the city to enjoy the gruesome spectacle and for it to serve as due warning to those who might transgress the written law, the gallows needed to be positioned on the highest point in the city, which is the area more or less where Williamson Park now stands. Some even say Ashton Memorial marks the actual spot of the gallows, others feel it more likely to have been somewhere behind the monument. Until my subsequent research I knew nothing of these things... armed with this information everything slowly began to make a little more sense.

Many people, including quite a few of the unfortunate victims of the Pendle Witch Trials, lived their last moments right up on that hill, along with countless others accused and found guilty of frequently the most derisory of crimes.

This is long before the Williamson family decided to create, from what had by then become a quarry, their stunning transformation of the area into the exquisitely beautifully landscaped park we see there today.

I dowsed over countless maps, both modern and ancient attempting to get to the bottom of the building with the metal gates and found myself reaching a complete blank. No trace of such building evidenced as ever standing in that area through any bygone era. An obvious course of action would take me back to the location, this time better prepared, for a proper investigation. At the time of writing this in 2013, this has yet to happen, I am sure it will come about that I re-open the case one day…in the meantime the gated building eludes me finding it on any satellite or ordnance maps.

I want to emphasize, normally I do quite frequently find myself compelled to debunk alleged paranormal activity; of the cases I have encountered quite a percentage turn out to have perfectly rational explanations and my feeling is that this is exactly how things ought to be.

Yet there are a select few amongst all those cases I get involved with which do require my more interactive approach. Those places where I have been called in and there genuinely is a manifestation of some kind for me to deal with in my own particular way. Then again other situations where I happen to be in the right place at the right time, to undergo an immediate banishment or cleansing

MY CLIENT IS ME

Williamson Park is unique. In a sense I am effectively my own client. If looking into such a case for another client I would clearly examine all the evidence, asking myself initially if I am willing to trust the validity of the claims made and going on to ask many questions prior to committing to my own involvement. Then I generally dowse in private to establish if there is indeed a genuine spirit entity in the said location.

Treating myself here as my own client and examining all the evidence as I currently have it available, in the way I offer my usual verbal and written summarizing report to others, so I shall now go through this process for myself.

Clearly a paranormal experience occurred, and I am happy to 100% confirm my belief in this being the case. Having looked into the history of the area, I found years before it became a park it was known as Gallows Hill, the purpose of which existed to hang those unfortunate people found guilty in Lancaster Court of crimes punishable with death. It operated as such until 1800 and countless lives were lost in such a horrific way on that very hill.

Having distantly dowsed the area, I can confirm that a massive paranormal energy portal exists in the location. One which at the time of writing I am still pondering and ascertaining exactly how to seal or even if I actually have the right to…

Having been unable to locate on any maps or satellite images the exact location the experience occurred around, until a further visit on-site takes place I find it is impossible to validate that the derelict building exists there as any three-dimensional reality within our world. My instinct says I somehow temporarily entered into some kind of usually unseen netherworld which is where these unusual experiences occurred. For the moment though this remains only an educated guess.

As for the entity encountered, my feeling is it did not consist of entirely one single being. Although, again I emphasize until further evidence is collected through another on-site investigation, this is purely an educated supposition; and my supposition is that here we have collective souls joined together as one, all of whom suffered the same horrible fate. They are furiously angry and quite likely insanely so!

I know I have a duty of care to go back and learn more of this manifestation. Who knows, by the time you read this it may have already happened...and I will have re-visited and finally lain to rest my own nemesis.

MEETING MY NEMESIS PART TWO (2018)

I was certainly all too aware of what awaited me this time as I stepped out of my car and with deliberate footsteps made my way once more to face my nemesis…

****

Almost five years since my first terrifying adventure on that very hill, 2018 saw me duly parking my car on the carpark at Williamson Park, Lancaster, in Northwest England. Kiki had insisted that she come with me, I acquiesced but equally insisted she stay in the café for the duration of my new investigation to protect the most precious person in my life.

Truth be told, I had known for a while that the time fast approached for me to revisit. At last that crucial moment arrived. This time around though I arrived considerably better prepared…

A power-bracelet of purest turquoise adorned my left wrist, to lend me extra magical strength. Many years ago I followed a lucid dream to personally visit a previously uncharted ancient bronze-age quarry, all in the quest to locate a particular small piece of copper ore which had been revealed to me in that same dream. Copper is of the Goddess, and on this day I carried this very piece of copper ore right there in my pocket to protect me.

I also brought along my wooden dowsing pendulum. I have a few pendulums; my wooden one though feels to me the most connected with nature. Though I recognised it would be unlikely I would be afforded any precious opportunity to consult it, nevertheless it felt personally reassuring to know my pendulum was there, together with my camera, safely stowed away in my backpack if required.

Was I nervous and scared? Of course and quite a lot! Walking through the main thoroughfare of the park with Kiki I knew exactly where shortly to head. Foregoing a visit the café myself, I left Kiki in there, and after kissing her goodbye, I purposefully began my deviation off into the more wildly untamed area where I knew my destiny awaited me.

As I neared the location of my nemesis, I must admit that I kind of knew what to expect from the landscape.

THE GATES TO WHAT?

I came face to face with gates…

Although in precisely the same place as before, these were absolutely not the gates I had witnessed last time. Far more modern and efficient at keeping intruders out than those decaying gothic gates so committed to my memory.

But what lay hidden beyond these newer gates?

An overgrown reservoir stood clearly visible through the narrow railings. No decaying house and no possible way inside to investigate further. Not that I would have particularly wished to venture inside anyway!

What there were though were walls. Stood at two and half metres high to protectively and squarely lock-in the reservoir from anyone crazy enough to think it might be a great idea to explore it.

That I should find such a place came as no surprise to me whatsoever. Having already poured over so many maps seeking the derelict building, I could hardly fail to have noticed the reservoir sitting exactly where I felt the ruin ought to be.

This confirmed the theory which emerged through my subsequent surmising and dowsing since 2013.

The building around which I experienced such abject terror didn't exist as a three-dimensional place. Rather I somehow temporarily entered into a netherworld for a short time; and this is where I encountered the multi-faceted evilness of the being that chased me from out of this portal through the gothic gates.

Okay, so one theory now confirmed, what of the entity?

MEETING AN OLD "FRIEND"

Oh, the entity was still there all right!!!

This time though I didn't quite sense it laying there waiting ready to pounce and devour me. I needed to explore. I needed to face my nemesis in a measured way and even see if I might be able to communicate with it!

Walking slowly alongside the claustrophobic closeness of the first left-hand wall surrounding the reservoir it became like some cloying darkness was closing in all around me.

The feeling of unease still remained with me from before, although thankfully no paradigm shift in my reality happened for me this time…just a sense of foreboding as I reached the end of the left-hand wall.

The rear wall furthest from the gates next awaited me around this next right-hand corner. All too aware this is where everything had turned upside down for me once before, would the same unbearable maelstrom of oppressive negativity descend upon me when I turned that corner?

During any investigation one cannot allow fear in. For sure I was so scared my knees were trembling when I arrived on the day. Once getting started though I needed to put all that completely out of my mind to get on with what I went there for. Fear leaves us a gaping wide-open conduit for all kinds of paranormal nasties who just love adding extra fire to our inner fears and then enjoy feeding off the terror they create.

So before I walked around that corner to my destiny I took a few moments to put myself into a state of waking meditation, as I knew this would leave me highly protected and more importantly quell any of my own ego-based fear reactions…

You might well be wondering at this point why I hadn't done that five years before and so avoid all the ensuing drama that unfolded on that fateful day; and I would have to agree this is a perfectly reasonable question for you to ask. The honest answer is that back then I didn't actually know how to achieve a waking meditation!

We can only learn that which we are ready for…

The entity waited for me as I turned the corner. Perhaps because of my meditation or maybe because we were now meeting in my normal reality, I wasn't as unsettled as the last time we met face to face. For sure the presence was still thoroughly malevolent, also just as threatening and all the other sensations all too strongly etched into my memory from our previous encounter. This time I didn't feel there was the need to run and escape though.

Probing psychically outwards I sought to learn the nature of what exactly this presence was. Under normal circumstances something will come back to me when reaching outwards towards any spirit entities. This creature defied my attempt; the overriding feeling I got was of tortured pain and, as I earlier surmised, it consisted as an insane conglomerate of multiple once living people; all caught together through the shared experience of meeting their grizzly end up on Gallows Hill.

I spent over an hour investigating the location in 2018. Circling around those high walls countless times. The creature flitted in and out of my awareness as I walked. It didn't feel anything like as powerful as when we previously met. But then that last time this had seen me in all too real a sense existing temporarily within the creature's domain, venturing apparently through some kind of portal into a netherworld. I took many photos that day.

As I finally took my leave of Williamson for the last time I metaphorically shrugged my shoulders to mark this one down as just one more occasion where I simply couldn't really explain away all of what happened. If there is one thing I have learned through so many years of paranormal work and psychic healing is that I will occasionally encounter circumstances or situations regarded as mysteries beyond explanation.

Perhaps these moments are so alien to spirits having a human experience (I mean us!) that we have no practical reference points to help guide us to understand. And personally I find it quite reassuring to keep central in my mind that certain secrets of the arcane world will never be fully revealed to us or truly comprehended.

ONE TO ONE

Before we part company, I wanted us to enjoy a one to one chat, as I answer a few of the questions I typically get asked at my events.

How can I see a ghost? - My advice is to really be open to possibility and then leave the rest in the hands of the universe. There are some physical indications of being in the presence of a spirit entity. These include the feeling of static electricity around you, also a sense of someone unseen looking at you, and in some cases sneezing (this has happened to me on a few occasions) and personally a pain in my feet!

Having said all that, ghosts are not always dark shadow figures, or semi-translucent apparitions seen from out of the corner of an eye. Often they are attached to the most mundanely ordinary of locations as well. How do you really know the person walking towards you down that quiet country path can also be seen by others? Can you really vouch for sure that every single one of the faces viewed along the crowded city street is real in the sense we usually take for granted? If you believe you have never encountered a ghost don't be so sure. You might well have already experienced an infinite multitude of paranormal encounters and never even known it.

A regular question I get asked relates to healing and it usually goes something along these lines "Do any of us psychic/spiritual/natural healers possess some special gift to enable us to do what we do?" - I believe everyone possesses the latent ability to heal for themselves and others. Many of us have simply forgotten exactly how to do this. And I also believe healing cannot be taught as such. Those such as me can only help others to unlock their own empathic healing potential but it really is their honest seeking that will produce results for them.

Can you do a healing and/or investigate my ghosts for me? – I do truly wish I could help everyone who crosses my path. All those who contact me either directly or through email. I have to be selective in which cases I get involved with through necessity. If I took on every single case which came my way I would quite literally have no spare time for my family or to eat and sleep! When I cannot offer any of my direct help I will still intuitively do my best to advise and guide those seeking my services on how they might help themselves.

Do you wear any special clothes when on paranormal investigations or doing healings? – Not really. I opt for clothing which won't get in my way, so no long coats or scarves or anything else I might trip over. When distant or hands-on healing, wearing something loose fitting works best for me.

Do you have a team when you do an investigation? – I always work alone. I don't want to be preoccupied with the wellbeing of a team. This frees me to act instinctively through intuition.

You don't share too much about your lifestyle, how do you prepare for what you do? – I keep fit by walking, anaerobic workouts and running around haunted locations! I keep an open mind and use plenty of psychic self-protection. I like turquoise jewellery.

I'm an old-school astrologer, tarot reader and pendulum dowser. I have been pagan for most my adult life and a practising wizard since I was fifteen years old.

I know from life-experience that those paradigm shifting moments in life will usually require firstly the breaking down of established mindsets or lifestyle. My work as a public speaker embodies the message which lays hidden within my name.

Do you have any siblings and are they psychic? – I have three half-siblings. None of them have chosen to develop their psychic ability.

What is the biggest misconception about what you do? – That I am somehow special or have some gift which enables me to see things most people cannot and psychic heal. Everyone has the latent ability to do what I do. They have just ignored it for most of their lives!

Like unused muscles, any psychic potential we have will gradually diminish unless nurtured. I am fortune that far from being discouraged by my family as a psychic toddler, I instead found myself appreciated and so embraced an acceptance of my ability from an early age. This allowed me the freedom to organically grow into all that I am and do today

Where are you from? – I am originally from Manchester of Scottish, Irish and Scandinavian roots. I live with the love of my life Kiki in Northern England.

Can you recommend any books? – I prefer not to as I believe we all need to follow our intuition. The books I read as a teen by Dion Fortune and later those by Scott Cunningham taught me a lot and I do still re-read them from time to time.

THE SPIRITS AT JIM'S BAR (NOVEL)

Om Darke is asked in to investigate an ancient pub in Dover known as Jim's Bar. He promises to report only what he finds and under no circumstances do any exorcisms. A spirit in the cellar wishes to seriously harm him, but a promise is a promise…

Soon the stakes would become much higher as Darke finds himself on the top level of a car park infamous for suicides. A whirlwind of events sees him facing ghostly battalion of long-dead Roman Centurions, coming face to face with his own doppelganger and yet somehow gathering a team around him along the way.

Om and his new team find themselves guests of this mysterious Count at his Gothic Scottish Castle veritably infested with ghosts. Om and his team are unable to leave until they've met them all. Will they manage to escape the clutches of The Count or has Om finally bought the farm this time?

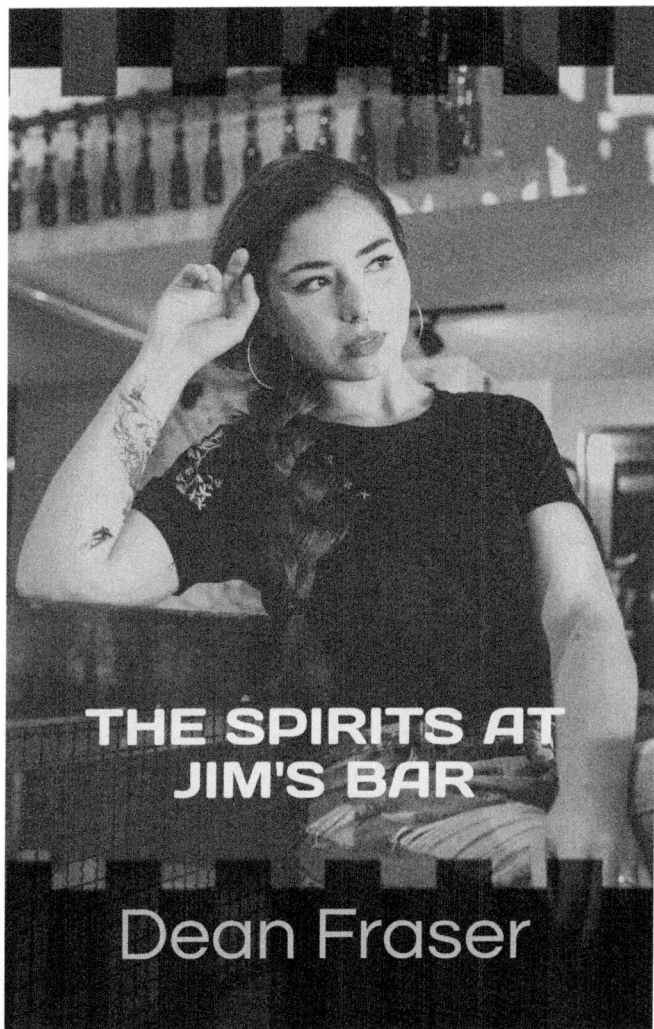

THE SPIRITS AT JIM'S BAR

Dean Fraser

THE COMPLETE UNLOCK YOUR LIFE WITH PENDULUM DOWSING

The author has shown over ten thousand people how to dowse over the last three decades plus, this book contains his four dowsing books all in the one set of covers; Anyone Can Dowse. Dowsing & Spiritual Healing, Dowsing & Crystal Healing and Born To Dowse.

The author proclaims If there is one thing his dowsing experience has proved over his years as a dowser, is when we are in harmony with our intuition life will take on unimaginable new meaning. Our dowsing pendulum is the perfect tool to achieve this!

Dean's books are available from Amazon, Barnes & Noble, Online Waterstones and all good book stores.

The Complete Unlock Your Life With Pendulum Dowsing

Dean Fraser

Printed in Dunstable, United Kingdom

71978458R00107